THE **JESUS** STORY

A BLENDING OF THE FOUR GOSPELS

THIRD PRINTING, 2021

COMPILED BY

BILL PERKINS

*From the original unique blending of
the Four Gospels by Johnston M. Cheney
and Stanley Ellisen, Th.D.*

White Horse Press

A DBA of White Horse Ministries

West Linn, Oregon

All Scripture quotations from the Gospels are original translations
by Johnston M. Cheney and Stanley Ellisen.

This book contains material from *Jesus Christ, the Greatest Life*,
a revised edition of *The Greatest Story*, in turn a revised edition of
The Life of Christ in Stereo.

Published by White Horse Press, a DBA of White Horse Ministries
West Linn, Oregon 97068

CONTENTS

PREPARATION
FOR MINISTRY

September 6 BC — April AD 29

The beginning of the glad news of Jesus the Messiah, the Son of God.

In the beginning was the Word. The Word was with God, and the Word was God. He was in the beginning with God.

All things were made through him, and nothing came into being without him. In him was life—life that was the light of mankind, shining in the darkness. And the darkness did not extinguish it.

(As a witness to the light, God sent a man named John to testify so that everyone could believe through him. John was not that light but came to tell about the light.)

The true light who enlightens everyone was coming into the world. He was in the world—a world made through him—yet the world did not recognize him. He came to his own creation, and his own people did not receive him. But to all who did receive him and put their trust in him, he gave the right to become children of God. These were born into God's family, not of blood or natural desire or human will, but of God.

The Word took on a human body and lived among us. We saw his glory—the glory of the one and only Son of the Father, full of grace and truth. (John testified about him: "This is the one of whom I spoke when I said, 'he who comes after me ranks before me. For he existed before me.'")

From his fullness we have all received blessing after blessing. The law came through Moses, but grace and truth came through Jesus Christ. No one has ever seen God, but the one and only Son who is close to the Father's heart—he has shown us what God is like.

The family record of Jesus Christ, the descendant of David, the son of Abraham: Abraham was the father of Isaac, and Isaac the father of Jacob, and Jacob the father of Judah and his brothers; Judah was the father of Perez and Zerah by Tamar, and Perez the father of Hezron, and Hezron of Ram, and Ram of Amminadab, and Amminadab of Nahshon, and Nahshon of Salmon, and Salmon of Boaz by Rahab, and Boaz of Obed by Ruth, and Obed of Jesse, and Jesse the father of David the King.

King David became the father of Solomon by the widow of Uriah, and Solomon the father of Rehoboam, and Rehoboam of Abijah, and Abijah of Asa, and Asa of Jehoshaphat, and Jehoshaphat of Jehoram, and Jehoram of Uzziah, and Uzziah of Jotham, and Jotham of Ahaz, and Ahaz of Hezekiah, and Hezekiah of Manasseh, and Manasseh of Amon, and Amon of Josiah, and Josiah the father of Jeconiah and his brothers about the time of the exile to Babylon.

After the exile, Jeconiah became the father of Shealtiel, and Shealtiel the father of Zerubbabel, and Zerubbabel of Abiud, and Abiud of Eliakim, and Eliakim of Azor, and Azor of Zadok, and Zadok of Achim, and Achim of Eliud, and Eliud of Eleazar, and Eleazar of Matthan, and Matthan of Jacob, and Jacob the father of Joseph, the husband of Mary, to whom was born Jesus, who is called Christ.

So there were fourteen generations from Abraham to David, another fourteen from David to the exile in Babylon, and another fourteen from the exile in Babylon to Christ.

Many have compiled partial accounts of the things prophesied and fulfilled among us—events confirmed to us by ministers of the Word who saw them take place from the beginning. Having carefully investigated the accuracy of those things from first to last, I felt constrained to write them out in consecutive order for you, my esteemed Theophilus, that you may be fully assured of the truths you have been taught.

In the days of King Herod of Judea, there was a priest named Zechariah who belonged to the priestly division of Abijah. His wife, a descendant of Aaron, was named Elisabeth. Both were righteous people in God's sight, living by the commands and rules of the Lord. They were childless, however, for Elisabeth was unable to have children, and both of them were elderly.

One day Zechariah was carrying out his duties as priest at the appointed time for his division. According to priestly custom, Zechariah's turn came to go into the temple of the Lord and burn incense. While all the people were praying outside, an angel of the Lord suddenly appeared to him, standing at the right side of the altar of incense. Zechariah was startled to see him, and fear overcame him. But the angel said, "Don't be afraid, Zechariah. Your prayer has been heard, and your wife, Elisabeth, will bear you a son.

You are to name him John. He will give you great joy and gladness, and many others will celebrate his birth. He will be great in God's sight. He is to take neither wine nor strong drink, and even from his conception he will be filled with the Holy Spirit.

"He will turn many in Israel to the Lord their God. He will go before the Lord in the spirit and power of Elijah, to turn the hearts of the fathers to their children, and sinners to the wisdom of the righteous— to prepare a people made ready for the Lord."

Then Zechariah said to the angel, "How can I be sure of this? I am an old man, and my wife is well along in years."

The angel answered him, "I am Gabriel, who stands in the presence of God. I have been sent to speak to you, to tell you this good news. But because you would not believe my words, which will come true at the right time, you will be silent and unable to speak until these things are fulfilled."

Meanwhile, the people outside were waiting for Zechariah and were surprised that he stayed so long in the temple. When he came out, he couldn't speak to them. The crowd understood that he had seen a vision in the temple because he made signs to them while remaining speechless.

Some time later, when his time of service was ended, he went home. Soon afterward his wife Elisabeth became pregnant and secluded herself for five months. And she said, "This is what the Lord has done for me, showing his concern by removing the disgrace I felt among my people."

In the sixth month, God sent the angel Gabriel to Nazareth, a town in Galilee, to a virgin named Mary. She was engaged to a man named Joseph, a descendant of David. The angel came to Mary and said, "Greetings, you who are richly blessed! The Lord is with you."

Mary saw him and was troubled by his greeting, wondering what it might mean. The angel said, "Don't be afraid, Mary, for you have found favor with God. Listen! You will become pregnant and will give birth to a son, whom you are to name Jesus. He will be great and will be called the Son of the Most High. The Lord God will give him the throne of his ancestor David and he will reign over the descendants of Jacob forever. His kingdom will never end."

"How is this possible," Mary replied, "since I am still a virgin?"

The angel responded, "The Holy Spirit will come upon you, and the power of the Most High will overshadow you. And so, the holy one born to you will be called the Son of God.

"And listen! Elisabeth, your relative, has conceived a son, even in her old age. She is already in her sixth

The Annunciation

month—she who was said to be unable to bear children! For with God, nothing is impossible."

"I am the servant of the Lord," Mary replied. "May what you have said truly happen to me."

Then the angel left her.

Then Mary hurriedly left for the hill country, to the city in Judah where Zechariah and Elisabeth lived. She came into Zechariah's home and greeted Elisabeth. As soon as Elisabeth heard Mary's greeting, the baby inside her jumped.

Elisabeth was filled with the Holy Spirit. "You are more blessed than all women!" she exclaimed. "And blessed is the child you will bear! Oh, why has God allowed the mother of my Lord to visit me? For when I heard your greeting, the baby inside me jumped for joy. You are so blessed for believing that what the Lord told you will really happen!"

Mary replied:

> *"My soul praises the Lord, and my spirit rejoices in*
> *God my Savior!*
> *For he has considered how humble his servant is.*
> *Yes, all future generations will call me blessed,*
> *for the Mighty One has done great things for me!*
> *Holy is his name!*
> *From generation to generation,*
> *His mercy is lavished on those who revere him.*

He has performed mighty deeds with his arm.
He has scattered those whose hearts are proud
  and brought down rulers from their thrones,
  but he has lifted up the humble.
He has filled the hungry with good things,
  but sent the rich away empty.
He has helped his servant Israel,
  remembering the mercy he promised
  to our ancestors—to Abraham
  and his descendants forever."

Mary stayed with her about three months, then returned home.

When the time came for Elisabeth to give birth, she delivered a son. Her neighbors and relatives heard about the abundant mercy the Lord had shown to her, and they joined with her in rejoicing.

After eight days they came to circumcise the baby. They began to call him Zechariah, after his father, but his mother insisted, "That is not his name. He is to be called John."

They objected, "But there is no one in your family by that name!" Then they began motioning to his father to see what he intended to name his son.

Zechariah asked for a writing tablet and wrote, "His name is John." All of them were astonished. At that moment, Zechariah regained his ability to speak and began to praise God.

As these events were reported throughout all the Judean hill country, everyone there grew afraid. They began to wonder, "What sort of child will this be?" And the Lord's favor rested on the child.

His father Zechariah was filled with the Holy Spirit and began to prophesy:

> "May the Lord God of Israel be blessed! He has visited and redeemed his people and has granted us a mighty salvation through the royal line of his servant David—just as he promised long ago through his holy prophets. He will save us from our enemies and from the snares of all who hate us. He will be merciful toward our fathers and will remember his holy covenant, the oath he swore to our father, Abraham. He will rescue us from the hands of our enemies so that we may serve him without fear in holiness and righteousness in his sight for as long as we live.

> "As for you, little one, you will be called the prophet of the Most High God. You will go before the Lord to clear a path for him, to give his people the knowledge of salvation in the forgiveness of their sins through the tender mercy of our God. His sunrise has dawned on us from above, shining on those sitting in darkness and in death's shadow. He will guide our feet in the way of peace."

And the child grew and became strong in spirit. Then he lived in the desert until the day of his introduction to Israel.

The birth of Jesus Christ happened like this: his mother, Mary, had been engaged to Joseph, but before they came together she was found to be pregnant through the Holy Spirit. Joseph—a just man who did not want to publicly shame her—considered whether he ought to divorce her quietly. But as he thought about these things, an angel of the Lord appeared to him in a dream and said, "Joseph, son of David, do not be afraid to take Mary home as your wife, because the baby in her womb is from the Holy Spirit. She will give birth to a son, and you are to call him Jesus, for he will save his people from their sins."

All this happened to fulfill the Lord's words spoken through the prophet: "Behold, a virgin shall conceive and bear a son, and they shall call him Immanuel" (meaning "God with us").

When Joseph awoke, he did what the angel of the Lord told him to do and took Mary home as his wife. But he had no intercourse with her until after she had given birth to a son, whom he named Jesus.

At that time a decree was issued by Caesar Augustus requiring the whole Roman world to register for a tax. (This first taxing occurred when Quirinius was

The Nativity

governor of Syria.) So everyone traveled to his home-town to be registered. Along with Mary (who was now pregnant), Joseph left Nazareth in Galilee and went to Judea to be registered in Bethlehem, the town of David (since he was descended from David). While they were there, the time came for her delivery, and she gave birth to her firstborn son. She wrapped him in strips of cloth and laid him in a manger because there was no room for them in the inn.

That night there were shepherds in the fields nearby who were watching over their flock. Suddenly an angel of the Lord stood beside them, and the glory of the Lord shone around them. They were terrified.

But the angel said to them, "Don't be afraid! For I bring you good news of great joy for everyone. Today in the city of David a Savior has been born to you—Christ the Lord. And this will be the sign for you: You will find the baby wrapped in strips of cloth and lying in a manger."

Suddenly with the angel a vast number of the heavenly host appeared, praising God and saying, "Glory to God in the highest! And on earth, peace to the people with whom he is pleased."

When the angels had returned to heaven, the shepherds said to each other, "Let's go to Bethlehem and see this mighty thing the Lord has told us about."

They hurried off and found Mary and Joseph and the baby, who was lying in a manger.

When they had seen this, they reported to everyone all that they had been told about this child. Those who heard the shepherds were amazed by the story. But Mary treasured these things in her heart, reflecting on what they might mean.

Then the shepherds went back, giving glory and praise to God for all they had heard and seen—which was exactly as they had been told.

Eight days later, at the child's circumcision, he was named Jesus, the name the angel had given him before he was conceived.

When the time for Mary's purification had ended (a period specified by the law of Moses), they brought Jesus to Jerusalem to present him to the Lord, as required by the law: "Every firstborn male will be set apart for the Lord." They came also to offer a sacrifice according to the law: "a pair of doves, or two young pigeons."

Now living in Jerusalem was a righteous and devout man named Simeon. He was waiting for the comforting of Israel, and the Holy Spirit was upon him. And the Holy Spirit had revealed to him that he would not die until he had seen the Lord's Messiah. The Spirit prompted him to go into the temple. When the parents brought in the child Jesus to comply with the custom of the law, Simeon took Jesus in his arms and praised God. Then he said, "Now, O Lord, allow your servant to depart in peace, according to your promise. For I have seen your salvation, which you have prepared in full view of everyone, a revealing light to the Gentiles and a glory to your people Israel."

Joseph and the mother of Jesus were astonished at what was said about him. Then Simeon blessed them, and to Mary he added, "This child is destined to cause the fall and the rising again of many in Israel and to be a sign that will be opposed. In that way, the thoughts of many hearts will be revealed—and a sword will pierce your own soul as well."

Also there was Anna, a prophetess, the daughter of Phanuel of the tribe of Asher. (Anna was very old. Her husband had died seven years after they were married, and she had lived as a widow for eighty-four years. She never left the temple but served God by fasting and praying night and day.) At that same moment, she came up and gave praise to the Lord, speaking about Jesus to everyone in Jerusalem who was looking for deliverance.

When Mary and Joseph had done everything required by God's law, they returned to Nazareth in Galilee, their hometown.

After Jesus was born in Bethlehem of Judea during the reign of King Herod, wise men from the East came to Jerusalem. "Where is the one who has been born king of the Jews?" they asked. "We saw his star in the East and have come to worship him."

When Herod heard about this, he grew anxious—and all Jerusalem with him. He called together all the chief priests and the teachers of the Jewish law and demanded to know where the Messiah was to be born.

"In Bethlehem of Judea," they replied. "For this is what the prophet wrote: 'You, Bethlehem in the land of Judah, are certainly not the least among the rulers of Judah; for out of you will come a ruler who will shepherd my people Israel.'"

Then Herod sent secretly for the wise men and asked them the exact time when the star had appeared. He then sent them on to Bethlehem. "Go," he said. "Search carefully for the young child. And when you have found him, bring word back to me. Then I, too, can come and worship him."

After hearing the king's instructions, the wise men left. And the star they had seen in the East went ahead of them until it stood over the place where the child was. Seeing the star, the wise men were overcome with joy.

As they entered the house, they saw the young child with Mary, his mother, and they bowed down and worshiped him. They opened their treasures and presented him with gifts: gold and frankincense and myrrh.

Then God warned them in a dream not to return to Herod. So they returned to their country by another route.

After the wise men departed, an angel of the Lord appeared to Joseph in a dream and said, "Get up and take the young child and his mother and flee to Egypt. Stay there until I bring you word, because Herod will hunt for the boy to kill him."

So Joseph got up and took the baby and his mother and left that night for Egypt. There they stayed until Herod died. This fulfilled what the Lord had spoken through the prophets: "Out of Egypt I have called my son."

When Herod realized he had been tricked by the wise men, he was enraged. He ordered the deaths in Bethlehem of all male babies two years old and younger (according to the time he had learned from the wise men). This fulfilled what was spoken by the prophet Jeremiah: "A voice is heard in Ramah, wailing and bitter mourning, Rachel weeping for her children; she refused to be comforted, because they were no more."

After Herod died, an angel of the Lord appeared in a dream to Joseph and said, "Get up and take the young child and his mother and go to the land of Israel. Those who wanted to kill the child are dead."

So Joseph got up and took the child and his mother and entered the land of Israel. But when he heard that Herod's son Archelaus was reigning in Judea, he was afraid to move there. Having been warned by God in a dream, he went on to the province of Galilee, and they made their home in the town of Nazareth. In this way, the prophets' words were fulfilled: "He will be called a Nazarene."

The young child grew and became strong and was filled with wisdom. God's favor rested upon him.

Every year Jesus' parents went to Jerusalem for the Feast of Passover. In accordance with this custom, they attended the feast when he was twelve years old. But when it was over and everyone was on the way home, the boy Jesus stayed behind in Jerusalem without his mother and Joseph knowing it. They assumed he was somewhere among the travelers, and they journeyed on for a day while looking for him among their relatives and friends. Still not finding him, they returned to Jerusalem, searching for him.

After three days they found him—in the temple, seated among the rabbis, listening to them and asking questions. And all who were listening to him were astonished at his understanding and answers.

His parents were astounded to find him there. His mother said to him, "Son, why have you treated us like this? Your father and I have been anxiously searching for you."

"Why were you searching for me?" Jesus answered. "Didn't you know I had to be in my Father's house?"

They did not understand what he was telling them. Nevertheless, he returned with them to Nazareth and was obedient to them. His mother, meanwhile, treasured all these things in her heart.

And Jesus grew in wisdom and stature and in favor with God and men.

Now in the fifteenth year of the reign of Tiberius Caesar (when Pontius Pilate was governor of Judea, Herod was ruler of Galilee, his brother Philip was ruler of Iturea and Trachonitis, Lysanias was ruler of Abilene, and Annas and Caiaphas were high priests), the word of God came to John, the son of Zechariah, in the desert.

In those days, John came into the region around the Jordan River in the Judean desert in fulfillment of what is written by Isaiah the prophet: "I send my messenger before you, to prepare a path for you." John preached the baptism of repentance for the forgiveness of sins.

He said, "Repent, for the kingdom of heaven is near."

This John the Baptist was the one spoken of by the prophet Isaiah: "The voice of one calling in the desert, 'Prepare the way for the Lord. Make straight paths for him! Every valley shall be filled up and every mountain and hill shall be leveled; crooked paths will be straightened and rough paths will be made smooth—and all mankind will see the salvation of God.'"

John wore clothing made of camel's hair with a leather belt around his waist. He ate locusts and wild honey.

People from Jerusalem and all of Judea and all around the Jordan went out to him. They confessed their sins and were baptized by him in the Jordan. When he saw the crowds, including many Pharisees and Sadducees, he said to them, "You children of snakes; who warned you to flee from the coming wrath? Produce the fruit that comes from repentance! Don't imagine you can say, 'Abraham is our father.' I'm telling you that God can raise up children for Abraham even from these stones! Even now the ax is ready at the root of the trees. Every tree that does not bear good fruit will be cut down and thrown into the fire."

So the crowds asked him, "What should we do?"

He answered, "Whoever has two tunics should share with someone who has none. Those who have food should do the same."

Tax collectors also came to be baptized, and they asked him, "Teacher, what should we do?"

He told them, "Take no more than is required."

Soldiers were also asking him, "What should we do?"

He said to them, "Don't extort money by threatening people, don't make false accusations against anyone, and be content with your pay."

With anticipation, the people began wondering if John might be the Messiah. He answered them all by saying, "I baptize you in water to show your repentance. But coming after me is someone greater than I—someone whose sandals I am not worthy to remove, someone whose sandal thong I am not fit to stoop down and untie! He will baptize you in the Holy Spirit and in fire. His winnowing fork is in his hand, and he will thoroughly clean his threshing floor and gather his wheat into the barn. But the chaff he will burn up with unquenchable fire."

With many similar exhortations, he was preaching good news to the people.

When all the people had been baptized, Jesus came from Nazareth to be baptized by John in the Jordan. But John tried to stop him. "I should be baptized by you," he said. "Why are you coming to me?"

"Let it be so now," Jesus answered. "It's appropriate that in this way we accomplish what is right." Then John agreed, so Jesus was baptized by John in the Jordan.

As Jesus came up out of the water and was praying, he saw the skies opened and the Holy Spirit of God descended on him in the form of a dove and rested on him. And a voice came from heaven: "You are my beloved Son. In you I take great delight!"

Now Jesus made his first public appearance at about age thirty. Although supposedly the son of Joseph, he was actually descended from Heli, who was the son of Matthat, the son of Levi, son of Melchi, son of Jannai, son of Joseph, son of Mattatha, son of Amos, son of Nahum, son of Esli, son of Naggai, son of Maath, son of Mattatha, son of Semein, son of Josech, son of Joda, son of Joanan, son of Rhesa, son of Zerubbabel, son of Shealtiel, son of Neri, son of Melchi, son of Addi, son of Cosam, son of Elmadam, son of Er, son of Joshua, son of Eliezer, son of Jorim, son of Matthat, son of Levi, son of Simeon, son of Judah, son of Joseph, son of Jonam, son of Eliakim, son of Melea, son of Menna, son of Mattatha, son of Nathan, son of David, son of Jesse, son of Obed, son of Boaz, son of Salmon, son of Nahshon, son of Amminadab, son of Admin, son of Ram, son of Hezron, son of Perez, son of Judah, son of Jacob, son of Isaac, son of Abraham, son of Terah, son of Nahor, son of Serug, son of Reu, son of Peleg, son of Heber, son of Shelah, son of Cainan, son of Arphaxad, son of Shem, son of Noah, son of Lamech, son of Methuselah, son of Enoch, son of Jared, son of Mahalaleel, son of Cainan, son of Enosh, son of Seth, the son of Adam, the Son of God.

Then Jesus, filled with the Holy Spirit, returned from the Jordan. Immediately the Spirit drove him into the desert with the wild beasts where he remained for forty days. The Spirit led him there to be tempted by the devil.

He ate nothing during that whole time. After fasting for forty days and nights, he was hungry. So the tempter, Satan, came to him and said, "Since you are the Son of God, command these stones to become loaves of bread."

Jesus replied, "It is written, 'Man shall not live on bread alone but on every word that comes from the mouth of God.'"

Then the devil took him into the holy city, Jerusalem, and set him on top of the temple. "Since you are the Son of God," he said, "throw yourself down from here. For it is written, 'he will command his angels to guard you and carry you in their hands, lest you injure your foot on a rock.'"

Jesus replied, "It is also written, 'You are not to tempt the Lord your God.'"

Then the devil took him to a very high mountain. In a single moment, he showed Jesus all the kingdoms of the world and their glory. And he said to him, "All this power and splendor I'll give to you—it has been turned over to me, and I can give it to whomever I want. So bow down and worship me, and it will all be yours."

Jesus replied, "Be gone, Satan! For it is written, 'Worship the Lord your God and serve him only.'" So the devil, after trying every kind of temptation, left Jesus until an opportune time. And angels came and ministered to him.

When the Jews sent priests and Levites from Jerusalem to ask John, "Who are you?" He did not hesitate to tell them, "I am not the Messiah."

"Then who are you? Are you Elijah?" they asked.

"No, I am not," he replied.

"Are you then the prophet?"

"No," he answered.

"We need to report back to those who sent us," they insisted. "Tell us—who are you? What do you say about yourself?"

John replied, "I am a voice calling in the desert, 'Make a straight path for the Lord,' as the prophet Isaiah said."

Some questioners sent from the Pharisees asked John, "Then why are you baptizing, if you are not the Messiah, nor Elijah, nor the prophet?"

John answered, "I baptize in water, but there is one standing among you whom you do not know. Although he comes after me, he ranks ahead of me. I am not fit even to untie his sandal thong." This happened in Bethany, beyond the Jordan River where John was baptizing.

The next day John saw Jesus coming towards him and he exclaimed, "Look! The Lamb of God who takes away the sin of the world! This is the one about whom I said, 'One is coming after me who ranks ahead of me'—for he existed before me. I had not known him. But the reason I came to baptize was so that he might be made known to Israel."

John also declared, "I saw the Spirit coming down from heaven like a dove and resting on him. And though I had not known him, the one who sent me to baptize said to me, 'The one on whom you see the Spirit come down to rest—he is the one who will baptize in the Holy Spirit.' And I have seen and I have testified this is the Son of God."

John was standing, the next day, with two of his disciples. As Jesus walked past, John said, "Look! The Lamb of God!" When the two disciples heard him say this, they began following Jesus.

Jesus turned and saw them coming after him. "What are you seeking?" he asked.

"Rabbi," they said, "where are you staying?" (Rabbi means "teacher.")

He answered, "Come and see."

They went and saw where he was staying and spent that day with him (from about ten o'clock in the morning).

Andrew, Simon Peter's brother, was one of these two who heard John speak and who followed Jesus. The first thing Andrew did was to find his brother, Simon, and tell him, "We have found the Messiah!" (Messiah means "the Christ.")

Andrew brought him to Jesus. Jesus looked closely at him and said, "You are Simon, the son of John? You will be called Cephas" (which means "a stone").

The next day Jesus decided to travel into Galilee. He found Philip (who was from Bethsaida, the same town Andrew and Peter were from) and said to him, "Follow me."

Philip went to Nathanael and said to him, "We have found the one of whom Moses and the prophets wrote—Jesus, the son of Joseph, from Nazareth."

"Can anything good come out of Nazareth?" Nathanael said.

"Come and see," Philip answered.

When Jesus saw Nathanael approaching, he said, "Look! Here is a truly honest Israelite!"

Nathanael said to him, "How do you know me?"

"Before Philip called you—while you were under the fig tree—I saw you."

"Rabbi, you are the Son of God!" Nathanael exclaimed. "You are the king of Israel!"

Jesus answered, "You believe because I said I saw you under the fig tree? You will see bigger things than these!" And he continued: "I tell you the truth—and I tell this to both of you—the time is coming when you'll see heaven opened and the angels of God ascending and descending on the Son of Man."

On the third day, there was a wedding in Cana, a village of Galilee. Jesus' mother was there, and Jesus and his disciples also were invited. When the wine ran out, Jesus' mother said to him, "They have no wine."

"Dear woman," Jesus replied, "why have you come to me? My time is not yet here."

His mother instructed the servants, "Whatever he tells you to do, do it."

Six large water jars were standing nearby (for use in Jewish ceremonies of purification), each holding about twenty to thirty gallons. Jesus said to the servants, "Fill the jars with water." So they filled them up to the brim. Then he told them, "Now draw some out and take it to the banquet host." And this they did.

The banquet host tasted this water that had turned into wine, not knowing where it came from (though the servants who had drawn the water knew). Then he called the bridegroom and said, "Everyone puts out the good wine first, and the cheaper wine comes after the guests have drunk freely. But you have saved the best wine until now!"

And so it was that in Cana of Galilee Jesus performed his first miracle and displayed his glory, and his disciples trusted in him.

Then Jesus went down to Capernaum with his mother and brothers and his disciples, and they stayed there a few days.

THE FIRST YEAR
OF MINISTRY

April AD 29 — March AD 30

As the Passover of the Jews approached, Jesus went
up to Jerusalem. In the temple he found men selling cattle and sheep and doves, and others sitting at
tables exchanging money. So he made a whip out of
cords and drove them all out of the temple and their
sheep and cattle with them. Then he dumped out the
coins of the moneychangers and overturned their
tables. And to those who sold doves he said, "Take all
this out of here! Don't make my Father's house into
a market!" His disciples remembered the Scripture,
"Passion for your house has consumed me."

The Jews spoke up to Jesus. "Since you are doing
these things," they said, "what miraculous sign

will you show us?"

Jesus answered, "Destroy this temple, and in three days I will raise it up."

"This temple has taken forty-six years to build," the Jews replied, "and you will raise it up in three days?"

But Jesus was speaking of the temple of his body. After he was raised from the dead, his disciples remembered him saying this, and they believed the Scripture and what he had said.

While Jesus was in Jerusalem at the Passover, many believed in him when they saw the miracles he did. But Jesus didn't entrust himself to them. He understood people; he needed no one to tell him about them because he knew what was in them.

A Pharisee named Nicodemus, a ruler of the Jews, came at night to see Jesus. "Rabbi," said Nicodemus, "we know you're a teacher sent by God because no one can do the miracles you do unless God is with him."

"I tell you the truth," Jesus answered, "unless someone is born from above, he cannot see the kingdom of God."

"How can a person be born when he is old?" Nicodemus asked. "He can't enter again into his mother's womb to be born, can he?"

"I tell you the truth," Jesus said, "unless a person is born of water and the Spirit, he cannot enter the kingdom of God. The flesh gives birth to flesh while the Spirit gives birth to spirit. Don't be surprised that I said, 'You must all be born from above.' The wind blows wherever it wants to and you hear its sound, but you don't know where it's coming from or where it's going. That is how it is with everyone who has been born of the Spirit."

Nicodemus replied, "How is all this possible?"

Jesus answered, "You're the teacher of Israel, and yet you don't understand this? I tell you the truth, we speak about things we know and testify about what we have seen—yet you people still do not accept what we say! I've told you about earthly things and you don't believe. How then will you believe if I tell you about heavenly things?

"No one has risen into heaven except the one who came down from heaven—the Son of Man. Just as Moses lifted up the serpent in the desert, in the same way the Son of Man must be lifted up. And whoever believes in him will receive eternal life. For God loved the world so much that he gave his only Son, that whoever believes in him should not perish but have eternal life.

"God did not send his Son into the world to condemn the world but to save the world through him. Whoever believes in him will never be condemned, but whoever refuses to believe stands condemned already because he has failed to believe in God's one and only Son.

"The verdict is this: The light has come into the world, but people loved darkness rather than the light because their deeds were evil. Everyone who practices evil hates the light and doesn't come to the light, for he is afraid to have his deeds exposed. But whoever practices the truth comes into the light so his deeds may be fully revealed for what they are—deeds done through God."

Afterward Jesus went with his disciples into the Judean countryside where he stayed with them awhile and baptized.

John was also baptizing in Aenon near Salim. Water was abundant there and people kept coming and being baptized, for John had not yet been thrown into prison.

A dispute developed between John's disciples and some Jews about purification rites. They approached John and said, "Rabbi, the one who was with you by the Jordan, the one you testified about—he is baptizing, and everyone is going to him."

John answered, "A man can take nothing except what heaven gives him. You yourselves can testify to what I said, that I am not the Messiah but was sent to introduce him. It's the bridegroom who marries the bride. The friend of the bridegroom waits and listens for him and is full of joy when he hears his voice. That is why my joy is now overflowing! He must increase in stature, while I move to the sidelines.

"The one who comes from above is over all. A person from earth belongs to the earth and speaks about the earth, but the one who comes from heaven is over all. He testifies to what he has seen and heard, yet no one accepts his testimony. The one who does accept his testimony insists that God is truthful because the one whom God has sent speaks the very words of God.

"God does not give his Spirit in a miserly way; the Father loves the Son and has placed everything in his hands. The one who believes in the Son has eternal life. The one who refuses to obey the Son will never see life; instead, God's wrath remains on him."

John rebuked the ruler Herod about Herodias, his brother Philip's wife, and about all the other evil things he had done. Then the king added insult to injury by throwing John into prison.

Jesus left Judea and returned to Galilee at that time, after learning that John had been arrested and that the Pharisees knew he was gaining and baptizing more disciples than John (though it was Jesus' disciples who were baptizing, not Jesus himself).

Now he had to travel through Samaria, so he came to a Samaritan village named Sychar, located near the plot of land Jacob had given to his son Joseph. Jacob's well was there and because he was weary from traveling, Jesus sat down by the well. It was about the sixth hour.

A Samaritan woman came to draw water, and Jesus said to her, "Will you give me a drink?" (His disciples had gone into the city to buy food.)

"You're a Jew, aren't you?" she replied. "How is it that you would ask for a drink from me, a Samaritan woman?" (The Jews avoid all contact with Samaritans.)

Jesus answered, "If only you had known the gift of God and who it is who says to you, 'Give me a drink,' you would have asked him for a drink instead, and he would have given you living water."

"Sir, you have nothing to draw with, and the well is deep. Where do you expect to get this 'living water'? Are you greater than our ancestor Jacob? He was the one who gave us the well and drank from it himself, as did his sons and his cattle."

"Everyone who drinks this water will thirst again," Jesus said. "But everyone who drinks the water I give him will never thirst again. Instead, the water I give him will become a fountain within him, springing up to eternal life."

Jesus and the Woman of Samaria

"Sir, give me this water so I won't be thirsty anymore or have to come here to draw water," the woman said.

"Go get your husband," Jesus replied, "then come back here."

"I don't have a husband," the woman answered.

"You're right in saying you don't have a husband," Jesus said, "because you have had five husbands—and the one you're living with now is not your husband. You have admitted the truth."

"Sir," the woman replied, "it's clear to me that you're a prophet. Our ancestors worshiped God on this mountain, yet you Jews say Jerusalem is the only proper place to worship."

"Believe me, woman," Jesus said, "the time is coming when you will worship the Father neither on this mountain nor in Jerusalem. You Samaritans don't know what you worship; we know what we worship, for salvation comes from the Jews. But the time is fast approaching, and has even arrived, when those who truly desire to worship will worship the Father in spirit and in truth. Those are the kind of worshipers the Father seeks. God is spirit, and those who worship him must worship in spirit and in truth."

The woman said, "I know Messiah is coming, the one who is called Christ. When he comes, he will tell us everything."

Jesus answered, "I am he—I who speak to you now."

Just then his disciples returned from the village, and they were surprised to find him talking with a woman. Yet none of them asked, "What are you doing?" or "Why are you talking with her?"

The woman left her water jar and went into the village and said to the men, "Come and meet a man who told me everything I ever did! This must be the Messiah!" So they left the village and went out to meet him.

Meanwhile, his disciples were urging him to eat. But he said to them, "I have food that you know nothing about."

The disciples began to ask one another, "Did anyone bring him something to eat?"

Jesus said to them, "My food is to do the will of him who sent me and to accomplish his work. Don't you say it's yet four months until the harvest? But look, I tell you! See the fields—they are already ripe for harvest! The one who reaps will receive a reward and will gather the fruit of everlasting life, so both the one who sows and the one who reaps will be glad together. The saying is true, 'One sows and another reaps.' I sent you to reap what you didn't work for. Others have worked, and you've started sharing in their labor."

Many of the Samaritans in that village believed in Jesus through the testimony of the woman who said, "He told me everything I ever did!" When the Samaritans found him, they begged him to stay with them, so he remained there for two days.

Many more believed because they heard him for themselves, and they said to the woman, "We don't believe anymore simply because of what you said. We've now heard him for ourselves, and we're convinced this is truly the Savior of the world!"

After two days Jesus left the village and traveled to Galilee because even he admitted that a prophet is not honored in his hometown. When he arrived in Galilee, the Galileans welcomed him, since they had attended the feast in Jerusalem and had seen the things he did there. So he returned to Cana in Galilee where he had turned the water into wine.

A certain royal official in Capernaum had a son who was ill. When he heard that Jesus had arrived in Galilee from Judea, he searched him out and begged him to come down and heal his son, who was about to die.

Jesus said to him, "Unless you people see miracles and wonders, you refuse to believe."

The official replied, "Sir, please come down before my child dies!"

Jesus answered, "Go—your son is living."

The man believed what Jesus said and left immediately. Even as he was returning home, his servants met him and reported, "Your son is alive!" He asked them when he began to get better.

"The fever broke yesterday, at the seventh hour," they replied.

The father knew that this was the exact time Jesus told him, "Your son is living." And he and all his household believed.

This was the second miracle Jesus performed after his return to Galilee from Judea.

Jesus returned to Galilee in the power of the Spirit, and news about him spread to the whole region. He began to teach in their synagogues, being praised by everyone.

Then he went to Nazareth, where he grew up, and visited the synagogue on the Sabbath, as was his custom. When he stood up to read, a scroll of the prophet Isaiah was handed to him. He unrolled the scroll and found the place where it was written: "The Spirit of the Lord is on me; because of this he has anointed me. He has sent me to preach good news to the poor, to proclaim freedom to the captives and recovery of sight to the blind. He has sent me to free the oppressed and to announce the year of the Lord's good favor."

With that, he rolled up the scroll, returned it to the attendant, and sat down. Every eye in the synagogue was on him. Then he said, "This very day this Scripture has been fulfilled in your presence."

They all spoke well of him and were in awe of his beautiful words. Then they said, "Isn't this Joseph's son?"

He replied, "Doubtless you will quote me the proverb, 'Physician, heal yourself. The things you did in Capernaum, do here in your hometown as well.' I tell you the truth, no prophet is honored in his hometown. You know there were many widows in Israel in Elijah's day when a drought parched the land for three-and-a-half years and a great famine followed. But Elijah wasn't sent to any of them except a widow of Zarephath in Sidonia. And don't forget that there were many lepers in Israel during the prophet Elisha's day, but none were healed except Naaman the Syrian."

When those in the synagogue heard these words of Jesus, they became furious. They rose up and forced him out of the city, leading him to the brow of the hill on which the city was built, intending to hurl him over the cliff. But Jesus walked through the middle of the crowd and went his way.

Jesus then left Nazareth and stayed at Capernaum, a city in Galilee located by the sea in the region of Zebulun and Naphtali. He did this so the words of Isaiah the prophet might be fulfilled: "The land of Zebulun and Naphtali, by the sea across from the Jordan—in Galilee where the Gentiles live—the people sitting in darkness have seen a bright light, and on those living in the land of the shadow of death, a light has dawned."

From that time on Jesus began to preach the gospel of God. "The time has arrived for the kingdom of God to come," he said. "Repent and believe the good news because the kingdom of heaven is near!"

Walking by the Sea of Galilee, Jesus saw Simon, called Peter, and his brother Andrew casting a net into the sea, for they were fishermen. Jesus told them, "Come and follow me, and I will make you into fishermen of people!"

Immediately, they left their nets and followed him.

Going on from there, he soon saw two other brothers, James and John, the sons of Zebedee. They were in a boat with their father, mending their nets. He called them, and immediately they left their father in the boat with the hired helpers and began to follow Jesus.

As soon as they came to Capernaum, Jesus entered the synagogue on the Sabbath and began to teach. A man with a spirit of an unclean demon was there, and the demon cried out, "Leave us alone! What are you doing to us, Jesus of Nazareth? Have you come to destroy us? I know who you are—the holy one of God!"

Jesus rebuked the demon, "Be quiet, and come out of him."

After the demon had knocked the man to the floor, thrown him into convulsions, and cried out with a shriek, it came out of the man without harming him.

They were all aghast and asked each other, "What's going on here? What new teaching is this? What amazing words—with authority and power so great that he commands even demons, and they obey him and come out!"

His fame spread at once through all the region of Galilee.

Jesus stood up and left the synagogue and went with James and John to the home of Simon Peter and Andrew. Simon's mother-in-law was sick in bed with a high fever, and they begged him to do something for her.

So he went to her bedside, touched her hand, and ordered the fever to subside. Then he took her hand and helped her rise up. Immediately the fever vanished, and she got up and began to wait on them.

When evening came and the sun set, everyone in the town with friends and relatives who were sick or diseased—and the demonized as well—brought them to him. He laid his hands on each of them and healed them all. With a single word he also cast out the demons. In this way the words of the prophet Isaiah were fulfilled: "He took up our sicknesses and removed our diseases." It seemed as if the whole city was at the door.

The demons who came out shouted, "You're the Son of God!" But he told them to be quiet and wouldn't let them speak, because they knew he was the Messiah.

Early the next day, long before sunrise, he got up and went by himself to a secluded spot where he could pray. Simon and the others were searching for him, and when they found him they said, "Everyone is looking for you."

But he responded, "Let's go to the other towns nearby so I can preach there, too. After all, that is the reason I'm here."

The crowds still searched for him, and when they found him, they tried to keep him from leaving. But he told them, "I have to preach the kingdom of God to the other cities, too. That is the very reason I was sent here."

Jesus traveled throughout Galilee, teaching in the synagogues and preaching the good news of the kingdom. He healed every sickness and disease that plagued the people and also cast out many demons.

The people crowded around him to hear the word of God as he was standing by the Lake of Gennesaret. He saw two boats moored by the shore belonging to some fishermen who were washing their nets. He got into one of the boats owned by Simon and asked him to push out a little way from the shore. Then he sat down and began to teach the crowds from the boat.

When he was finished, he told Simon, "Move out to the deep water and let down your nets for a catch."

"Master, we have worked hard all night and have caught nothing," Simon answered. "Nevertheless, because you have told me to do it, I'll let down the net."

As soon as they let down the net, they caught a huge number of fish—so many that the net began to break. They motioned to their partners in the other boat to come and help them, and both boats became so full of fish that they began to sink.

When Simon Peter saw what had happened, he fell down at Jesus' knees and said, "Leave me, Lord,

Jesus Preaching at the Sea of Galilee

for I am a sinful man!" He was astonished at the quantity of fish they had caught; so were his partners, the sons of Zebedee (James and John), as well as everyone else with them.

"Don't be afraid," Jesus said to Simon. "From now on you will catch people."

When they returned the boats to shore, they left everything and followed him.

While Jesus was in one of the cities, a man with leprosy saw him and came closer to plead with him. He knelt down, fell on his face, and worshiped him. "Lord," he said, "if you want to, you can make me clean."

Jesus was moved with compassion. He reached out and touched the man, saying, "I am willing; be cleansed." Instantly the leprosy was gone.

Then Jesus sternly warned the man and sent him away, saying, "Don't tell anyone what happened. Instead, go to the priest and show him your healed body. Then give the offering Moses commanded for your cleansing, so they will know what has happened."

But the man went out and spoke freely about this, spreading the news far and wide. Jesus' fame increased all the more, making it impossible for him to go openly into a city. Instead he had to remain in isolated places. Large crowds were assembling from everywhere to hear Jesus and be healed of their sicknesses.

Jesus continued, however, to slip away into the desert to pray.

After several days, Jesus returned to Capernaum. While he was teaching one day, some Pharisees and teachers of the law from all over Galilee and Judea and Jerusalem came and sat nearby. As soon as word spread that he had returned home, a large crowd gathered—so large that there was no room left even by the door. He was teaching them the word and healing them through the Lord's power.

Then four men tried to bring to Jesus a paralyzed man lying on a mat. (They were carrying him on the mat.) They couldn't get near Jesus because of the crowd, so they climbed to the housetop and tore open the roof directly above Jesus. They lowered the man on his mat, down through the tiles and right in front of Jesus. When he saw their faith, Jesus said to the paralytic, "Take heart, young man. Your sins are forgiven."

But the teachers of the law and the Pharisees began to object in their minds, "Who is this who dares to speak such blasphemy? Why does this man say such things? Who can forgive sins—but God alone?"

Jesus immediately knew their thoughts. "Why do you wonder about these things?" He said. "Why do you think such evil in your hearts? Which is easier, to tell this paralytic, 'Your sins are forgiven,' or to tell him, 'Get up, pick up your mat, and walk'?

"But in order that you may know the Son of Man has authority on earth to forgive sins," and here he spoke to the paralytic, "get up, pick up your mat, and go home."

Instantly the man got up in front of everyone. He picked up his mat and went home, praising God all the way. All who saw what happened were astonished, and they glorified God who had given such power to men. Everyone was awestruck and said, "We've never seen anything like this! We've seen incredible things today."

Afterward Jesus left that place and walked by the seashore. People kept coming to him and he taught them.

As he was passing by, he saw a tax collector named Levi (Matthew), the son of Alphaeus, sitting in his tax office. Jesus said to him, "Follow me," and Levi got up, left everything, and followed him.

Levi held a large banquet for Jesus in his home. As Jesus reclined to eat, he was joined by his disciples and a large number of tax collectors and other people of low reputation. (There were many of these people following Jesus.) When the Pharisees and the teachers of the law saw him eating with these tax collectors and other outcasts, they began speaking critically to his disciples: "Why do you eat and drink with tax collectors and sinners? And why does your teacher?"

When Jesus heard what they were saying, he replied, "It isn't people who are well who need a doctor, but those who are sick. You ought to go and learn what this means; 'I desire mercy, not sacrifice.' I haven't come to call the righteous; I have come to call sinners to repentance."

At that time the disciples of John, as well as those of the Pharisees, were fasting. John's disciples approached Jesus and asked, "Why do we and the disciples of the Pharisees frequently fast and make requests, while yours do not? They continue to eat and drink!"

Jesus replied, "How can you make the young men in a wedding party fast? How could they possibly mourn while the bridegroom is with them? But the time is coming when the bridegroom will be taken away from them. When that time comes, they will fast."

He also told them a parable: "Nobody sews a piece of new, unshrunk cloth on a tattered piece of clothing. If they did, the patch would pull away from the old garment and a worse tear would result. It would tear the new cloth, and the new piece wouldn't match the old. In the same way, nobody puts new wine into old wineskins, because the new wine would rupture the skins and spill out, and the wineskins would become useless. No, new wine must be put into new wineskins; in that way both the wine and the skins will be preserved. Also, nobody wants new wine after drinking the old. No, 'The old is better,' he says."

THE SECOND YEAR
OF MINISTRY

April AD 30 — March AD 31

On the first Sabbath of Jesus' second year of ministry, he was passing through the grain fields with his disciples. As they became hungry, they began to pluck some heads of grain, rub them in their hands, and eat them. When some of the Pharisees saw what they were doing, they said to him, "Why are your disciples breaking the Sabbath law?"

Jesus replied, "Haven't you read what David did when he and his men were hungry? He went into God's house when Abiathar was the high priest and ate the consecrated bread—which belongs to the priests only—and gave some to those with him. Or haven't you read in the law how the temple priests violate the Sabbath and yet remain guiltless? I tell you that someone greater than the temple is here. Had you only known what this means, 'I desire mercy and not sacrifice,' you would never have condemned the innocent.

"The Sabbath was made for mankind," he continued, "not mankind for the Sabbath! So then the Son of Man is Lord also of the Sabbath."

On another Sabbath, after he left that place, he returned to the synagogue to teach. A man with a crippled right hand was there, and the teachers of the law and Pharisees were watching Jesus. They wanted to see if he would heal the man on the Sabbath, so they could accuse him.

They asked Jesus, "Is it legal to heal on the Sabbath?"

He knew what they were thinking. He said to the man with the crippled hand, "Get up and stand in front of them." So the man stood up.

Then Jesus said to the others, "I also have a question for you. Is it legal on the Sabbath to do good, or to do evil? To save life, or to destroy it?"

But they kept silent. So he said, "Who among you would not rescue one of his sheep that happened to fall into a pit on the Sabbath? And yet a man is worth far more than a sheep! Therefore it is certainly legal to do good on the Sabbath." In anger he looked around at them all. He was grieved by the hardness of their hearts.

Then he said to the man, "Stretch out your hand."

The man extended it—and it became just as strong as his other hand.

This infuriated the others there, and they began discussing with one another what they might do to Jesus. The Pharisees went out and immediately held a council with the Herodians to plan how they might destroy him.

Jesus knew this and left there, traveling with his disciples to the sea.

Huge crowds followed Jesus from Galilee, the Decapolis, Jerusalem and all Judea, Idumea, and from regions across the Jordan, and his fame spread throughout Syria. People brought to him those who were sick or plagued with any disease or pain, as well as the demonized and epileptics and paralytics. Jesus healed them all.

A large crowd from the seacoast near Tyre and Sidon heard about what mighty things he was doing and came to him. He asked his disciples to get a boat ready for him in case the crowd grew too large. He had healed so many people that everyone who was ill or demonized pressed forward to touch him. When the demons saw him, they fell down in front of him and wailed, "You're the Son of God!" Yet he gave the demons strict orders not to reveal his identity. In this way the words of Isaiah the prophet were fulfilled:

> *"Consider my servant whom I have chosen,*
>   *the one I love, in whom I delight!*
> *I will put my Spirit upon him*
>   *and he will exercise justice among the nations.*
> *He will not quarrel or cry out,*
>   *nor will anyone in the streets hear his voice.*
> *He will not even break a bruised reed,*
>   *nor will he snuff out a smoldering wick,*
>   *until the time he leads justice to victory.*
>   *The nations will find great hope in his name."*

Then Jesus climbed a mountain and spent all night praying to God. At daybreak he called together a select group of his disciples. He named twelve of them apostles and called them to stay with him that he might send them out to preach. To them he gave power to heal every disease and sickness and to cast out demons.

The names of the twelve apostles are these: Simon (to whom he gave the name Peter); his brother Andrew; James and John, the sons of Zebedee (whom he also named Boanerges, meaning "the sons of thunder"); Philip; Bartholomew; Thomas; Matthew, the tax collector; James, the son of Alphaeus; Judas, the son of James (who was also called Thaddaeus); Simon (who was called the Zealot); and Judas Iscariot, who became a traitor.

Then he came down with them and stood in a level place. Many of his other disciples, as well as a large crowd of people, from all Judea, Jerusalem, and the coastal region of Tyre and Sidon, came to him there to hear him and to be healed. Everyone in the crowd kept trying to touch him because great power was coming from him and healing everyone.

When he saw the crowds, Jesus went up on the mountain and sat down. He looked at his disciples as they came to him, opened his mouth, and then began to teach.

"Blessed are you who are poor," he said, "for the kingdom of God is yours.

"Blessed are you who are hungry now, for you will be satisfied.

"Blessed are you who cry now, for you will laugh.

"But how terrible for you who are rich! You're enjoying the only comfort you'll get.

"How terrible for you who are full! One day you'll go hungry.

"How terrible for you who are carefree now! One day you'll weep and groan.

"How terrible for you who are spoken well of by others! For that is how their ancestors spoke of the false prophets.

"Blessed are those who are humble, for the kingdom of heaven belongs to them.

"Blessed are those who mourn, for they will be comforted.

"Blessed are the meek, for they will inherit the earth.

"Blessed are those who hunger and thirst after righteousness, for they will be filled.

"Blessed are those who show mercy, for they will receive mercy.

"Blessed are those whose hearts are pure, for they will see God.

"Blessed are those who make peace, for they will be called sons of God.

"Blessed are those who are persecuted for the cause of righteousness, for the kingdom of heaven belongs to them.

"Blessed are you when people hate you and curse you and persecute you and tell wicked lies about you because of me.

"Blessed are you when they excommunicate you and denounce you as evil, all because of the Son of

Man. Be glad when that happens and jump for joy, because great is your reward in heaven. For their ancestors did all these things to the prophets who lived before you.

"You are the salt of the earth. But if the salt has lost its saltiness, how can it become salty again? It's no longer good for anything except to be tossed on the ground and trampled underfoot.

"You are the light of the world. A city built on a mountaintop cannot be hidden, and no one lights a candle and puts it under a basket. Instead, we set it on a lampstand where it gives light for the whole house. In the same way you should let your light shine before other people, so they'll witness the good things you do and respond with praise to your Father in heaven.

"Don't imagine I came to do away with either the law or the prophets! I did not come to do away with them but to fulfill them. I tell you the truth, as long as heaven and earth exist, neither the smallest letter nor even part of a letter will be removed from the law until everything is fulfilled.

"That is why anyone who breaks even the least important of these commandments and teaches someone else to follow his example will be called the least important in the kingdom of heaven. The one who faithfully practices and teaches them, however, will be called great in the kingdom of heaven. I want you to know that unless your righteousness exceeds that of the teachers of the law and the Pharisees, you won't even enter the kingdom of heaven!

"You have heard that it was said to your ancestors, 'You are not to commit murder,' and 'Anyone who commits murder will have to answer to the court.' But I tell you that anyone who gets angry at his brother will have to answer to the court. And anyone who calls his brother 'empty-head' will have to answer to the Sanhedrin. And anyone who calls another 'You fool!' will be in danger of being thrown into hellfire.

"This means that if you're offering your gift at the altar and suddenly remember your brother has something against you, leave your gift at the altar and make it right with him. Then return and offer your gift.

"When you're heading to court with someone who has filed suit against you, try hard to reach a settlement before you arrive. Otherwise he may drag you to the judge, and the judge will hand you over to the police, and the police will throw you into jail. I tell you the truth, you won't get out of there until you've paid the last cent of what you owe!

"You have heard that it was said, 'You are not to commit adultery.' But I tell you that any man who even looks with sexual desire at a woman has already committed adultery with her in his heart. If your right eye causes you to fall into sin, pluck it out and throw it away! It would be better for one of your organs to be destroyed than for your whole body to be thrown into hell. Or if your right hand causes you to fall into sin, cut it off and throw it away! It would be better for a part of your body to be destroyed than for your whole body to be thrown into hell.

"It was said, 'If a man divorces his wife, let him give her a document of divorce.' But I tell you that if any man divorces his wife, except for marital unfaithfulness, he causes her to commit adultery. And anyone who marries a divorced woman commits adultery.

"You have heard that it was said to your ancestors, 'You are not to swear falsely,' and 'You must fulfill whatever vows you make to the Lord.' But I tell you not to swear at all. Don't swear an oath by heaven, for it is God's throne. Don't swear by the earth either, for it is his footstool. And don't swear by Jerusalem, for it is the city of the great king. Don't even swear by your head, because you can't make one hair white or black. When you say 'Yes,' mean 'yes,' and when you say 'No,' mean 'no.' Anything beyond this comes from the evil one.

"You have heard others say, 'An eye for an eye, and a tooth for a tooth.' But I am telling you not to resist an aggressor. If someone slaps you on the right cheek, allow him to slap the other one as well. If someone sues you and takes away your tunic, give him your cloak as well—and don't withhold your tunic from the person who takes your cloak. If someone forces you to go with him one mile, go two miles.

"Give to everyone who asks you for something, and don't refuse the person who wants to borrow from you. If anyone takes something that's yours, don't demand that he return it.

"You have heard others say, 'Love your neighbor and hate your enemy.' But I say to you, love your enemies and treat well those who mistreat you and bless those who curse you. Pray for those who abuse and persecute you. In that way you will be children of your Father in heaven. He makes his sun to rise on both evil and good people, and he sends rain on both the righteous and the unrighteous.

"What reward will you have, or what credit will be yours, if you love only those who love you? Even sinners love those who love them! Even tax collectors do that. Or if you greet only your friends, how does that make you different from anyone else? Don't even tax collectors do that?

"If you help only those who help you, what credit is that to you? Even sinners do that. Or if you give loans only to those whom you expect to repay you, what credit is that to you? Even sinners lend to sinners, to receive the same favor in return.

"No, you are to love your enemies, do good to them and lend to them, looking for nothing in return. Then you will have earned a handsome reward, and you will be children of the Most High God, because he is good even to those who are ungrateful and wicked.

"Since your Father is compassionate, you are to be compassionate. Since your Father in heaven is perfect, you are to be perfect.

"Be careful not to do your good deeds in front of others in order to be seen by them. If you do, you will earn no reward from your heavenly Father.

"When you give to the needy, don't blow a trumpet to announce it. That is what the hypocrites do in order to be applauded in the synagogues and on the street. I tell you the truth; they have already received their full reward. But when you give to the needy, don't let your left hand know what your right hand is doing. Give to the needy in secret. Then your

Father, who sees what is done in secret, will himself reward you.

"When you pray, don't act like the hypocrites. They love to pray while standing in the synagogues and on the street corners in order to be conspicuous to others. I tell you the truth, they have already received their full reward. Don't be like them. When you pray, go to a private room, close the door, and pray to your Father in secret. Then your Father, who sees what is done in secret, will reward you openly.

"And when you pray, don't practice empty repetition as the pagans do, thinking that so many words will cause them to be heard. Don't be like them! Your Father knows what you need even before you ask him. "So then, pray like this:

> *Our Father in heaven,*
>   *may your name be held in awe.*
> *May your kingdom come,*
>   *and may your will be done*
>   *on earth as it is in heaven.*
> *Give us the bread we need each day.*
> *And forgive us our sins,*
>   *as we also forgive those who sin against us.*
> *And do not allow us to be led into temptation,*
>   *but save us from the evil one.*

For yours is the kingdom, and the power,
  and the glory forever.
Amen.

"If you forgive those who offend you, your heavenly Father will also forgive you. But if you refuse to forgive those who offend you, then neither will your Father forgive you.

"And when you fast, don't put on a sad face like the hypocrites do. They wear somber faces to make sure everyone notices their fasting. I tell you the truth, they have already received their full reward. Don't be like them! When you fast, put oil on your head and wash your face so others won't know you're fasting. Yet your Father will see what you do in secret, and he will reward you.

"Do not store up for yourselves treasures on earth, where moths and rust destroy and where thieves break in and steal. Instead, store up for yourselves treasures in heaven, where neither moths nor rust destroy and where thieves cannot break in and steal. Your heart will be wherever your treasure is.

"The body's source of light is the eye, so if your eye is healthy your whole body will be filled with light. But if your eye is diseased your whole body will be filled with darkness. And if the light in your body is really darkness, how deep is that darkness!

"No one can serve two masters. Either he will hate one and love the other, or he will cling to one and despise the other. You cannot serve both God and riches.

"Therefore I say to you, don't worry about your life—what you should eat or drink—or about your body—what clothes you should wear. Doesn't life consist of more than what you eat, and isn't the body more than what you wear?

"Observe the birds. They don't plant crops or harvest them or store the produce in barns, yet your heavenly Father feeds them. Aren't you worth much more than birds?

"And tell me this, who of you by worrying can extend his life even a little? If you cannot do such a little thing as that, why do you worry about the rest?

"Why are you worried about clothing? Observe how the lilies grow. They don't work hard nor do they weave cloth, yet I tell you that not even Solomon in all his splendor was dressed like them. So if God gives plants such splendid attire—plants that are here today but tomorrow are thrown into a furnace—won't he clothe you even more richly, you people of little faith?

"That is why you shouldn't anxiously say, 'What is there to eat?' or 'What is there to drink?' or 'What is there to wear?' Do not doubt God's goodness. The people of the world seek desperately all these things, yet your heavenly Father knows full well that you need them. But first seek the kingdom of God and his righteousness, and these other things will be given you besides.

"So don't worry about tomorrow, because tomorrow will take care of itself. Today has enough trouble of its own.

"Also, do not judge others, otherwise you will also be judged. You'll be judged in the same way you judge others. If you don't condemn others, you won't be condemned. Forgive, and you'll be forgiven.

"Give and it will be given to you; a good amount, pressed down, shaken together, and running over will be poured into your lap. The same measure you use will be used for you."

Then he told them this parable: "Is it possible for a blind man to guide another blind man? Won't both of them fall into a pit? A disciple isn't greater than his teacher, and everyone who is fully taught will resemble his teacher.

"Why do you focus on a speck in your brother's eye but don't see the plank in your own? How can you

The Sermon on the Mount

say to your brother, 'Brother, allow me to remove the speck in your eye' when you don't even see the plank in your own eye? You hypocrite! First remove the plank from your own eye, and then you will be able to see clearly enough to remove the speck from your brother's eye.

"Don't give holy things to dogs, and don't throw your pearls in front of pigs—otherwise, they'll trample on them and turn around and injure you.

"Ask, and you'll receive. Seek, and you'll find. Knock, and the door will be opened for you. For everyone who asks, receives; and whoever seeks, finds; and the one who knocks will discover an open door.

"If your son should ask you for bread, who among you would give him a stone? Or if he asks for fish, will you give him a snake? Since, then, you know how to give good gifts to your children, how much more will your heavenly Father give good things to those who ask him!

"Treat others in the way you yourself would like to be treated. This sums up everything in the law and in the prophets.

"Enter through the narrow gate, because the gate is wide and the road is broad that leads to destruction. Many go that way! But the gate is narrow and the road is difficult that leads to life—and few are those who find it.

"Beware of false spokesmen for God who come to you disguised in sheepskin but are really ravenous wolves. You will recognize them by their fruit. Each tree is recognized by the kind of fruit it bears. People don't gather grapes from thorn bushes or figs from thistles, do they?

"No, every healthy tree produces good fruit, but a diseased tree produces rotten fruit. A healthy tree cannot produce rotten fruit, nor can a diseased tree produce good fruit. Every tree that fails to produce good fruit is cut down and thrown into the fire.

"A good person out of the good treasure in his heart produces good things, while the evil person out of the evil treasure in his heart produces evil things; each one speaks from whatever fills his heart. So indeed the fruit people produce will show you the kind of people they are.

"Why do you call me 'Lord, Lord!' but still refuse to do what I say? Not everyone who says to me 'Lord, Lord!' will be allowed to enter the kingdom of heaven. That is reserved for those who do what my heavenly Father desires.

"On that day many will say to me, 'Lord, Lord, didn't we prophesy in your name? Didn't we cast out demons in your name? And didn't we do many great things in your name?' Then without hesitation I will say to them, 'I never knew you. Get away from me, you who continually break the law!'

"But let me tell you what the person is like who hears and obeys me. He is like a wise man who dug deep down to the rock to lay the foundation for a house he was building. Then the rains came and the floodwaters rose and the winds howled and the storm battered that house. But it stood firm. It didn't collapse, because its foundation was firmly planted on the rock.

"On the other hand, whoever hears my teaching and fails to obey it is like a foolish man who built his house on the sand, without a foundation. The rains came and the floodwaters rose and the winds howled and the storm battered that house—and immediately it collapsed, completely ruined."

When Jesus finished speaking these words in the hearing of the people, the crowds were amazed at his message because he taught them as one who had authority and not as their teachers of the law.

When he had come down from the mountain, large crowds followed him, and he went to Capernaum.

A slave boy, who was dearly loved by the centurion who owned him, was very sick and near death. When the centurion heard that Jesus had come to Capernaum, he sent some Jewish elders to beg him to heal his servant, instructing them to say, "Lord, my servant lies paralyzed and in awful pain at home." When they came to Jesus, they begged him to act and said that the centurion was worthy of such a favor. "He loves our nation and built us our synagogue," they said.

So Jesus went with them, saying, "I will come and heal him."

As Jesus approached the house, the centurion sent friends to say, "Lord, don't trouble yourself, because I don't deserve to have you in my home and that's why I didn't think myself worthy enough to come to you in person. But if you will just say the word, my servant will be healed. I, too, am a man entrusted with authority and I have soldiers in my command. I say to one, 'Go,' and he goes, and to another, 'Come,' and he comes. I say to my slave boy, 'Do this,' and he does it."

Jesus was astonished to hear this. He turned and said to the crowds, "I tell you the truth, I have not found such extraordinary faith even in Israel! Many will come from all over to eat with Abraham and Isaac and Jacob in the kingdom of heaven, but the children of the kingdom will be thrown into the darkness outside. People there will be weeping and gnashing their teeth."

Then Jesus said to the centurion, "Go. Because you have believed, your request is granted." The man's servant was healed at that moment and when the messengers returned to the house, they found the slave boy completely well.

The next day he entered the village of Nain, accompanied by his disciples and a large crowd. When he approached the city gate, a dead man was being carried out, the only son of a widow. A large crowd from the city followed her. When the Lord saw her, he was filled with compassion for her.

"Don't cry," he told her. He walked to the coffin and touched it, and those carrying it stood still. He said, "Young man, get up!" The dead man sat up and began to speak, and Jesus gave him back to his mother.

Tremendous fear swept the crowds, and they began to praise God. "A great prophet has appeared among us!" they said, and, "God has visited his people!" Reports of this story circulated throughout Judea and the surrounding area.

While John was in prison, his disciples brought word of all the things the Messiah was doing. Then John summoned two of his disciples and sent them to Jesus, instructing them to ask him, "Are you the one who is coming, or should we look for someone else?"

When the men reached Jesus, they said, "John the Baptist sent us to ask you, 'Are you the one who is coming? Or should we look for someone else?'"

Right at that time, Jesus had healed many people suffering with diseases and illnesses, and the demonized. He also restored the sight of many who were blind. So Jesus said to them, "Go and report to John what you have seen and heard. Blind people have been given sight, crippled people are walking, people with leprosy are being healed, the deaf are hearing, the dead are being restored to life, and the poor are being told the good news. And blessed is the one who doesn't take offense because of me."

After John's messengers left, Jesus began to tell the crowd about John. "What did you go out into the desert to see?" he asked them. "A reed blown about by the wind? Of course not! What then did you go out to see? A man clothed in luxurious garments? Hardly! Those who wear expensive clothes and live in luxury stay in kings' palaces!

"So what did you go out to see? A prophet? Yes, I tell you—and much more than a prophet! He is the one of whom it was written, 'I am sending my messenger before you; he will prepare the way for you.'

"I tell you the truth, among those born of women, no prophet greater than John the Baptist has come

along. And yet even the lowliest person in the kingdom of heaven is greater than he."

(When the common people and tax collectors
heard him say these things, they admitted God's
ways were right, for they had been baptized by John.
But the Pharisees and the experts in the law rejected
God's purpose for themselves by refusing to be
baptized by John.)

"Since the time of John the Baptist until now,"
Jesus continued, "the kingdom of heaven suffers
violence, and violent men lay hold of it.

"All the prophets and the law prophesied until
the time of John. If you're willing to accept it, he
is Elijah who was predicted to come. If anyone has
ears to hear, let him hear!"

The Lord continued, "To what shall I compare
the people of this generation? What are they like?
They are like small children who sit in the marketplace and call to one another,

> 'We played the flute for you,
>   but you did not dance;
>   we sobbed, and you did not mourn.'

"I say this because when John the Baptist came,
he neither ate bread nor drank wine and you said
of him, 'he is demonized!' The Son of Man came

both eating and drinking and you say, 'Look! Here is a glutton and a drunkard, a friend of tax collectors and sinners!' Yet wisdom is always proved right [in all its products.]"

Then one of the Pharisees asked Jesus to come to dinner, so he went to his home and reclined at the table. After learning that Jesus was going to eat at the Pharisee's home, an outcast woman from the city brought an alabaster jar of ointment, and stood behind him weeping. She began to wash his feet with her tears and to wipe them with her hair, all the while kissing his feet and anointing them with the ointment.

When the Pharisee, who was his host, saw this, he thought, *If this man were really a prophet, he would know that this woman touching him is an immoral woman.*

"Simon," Jesus said to him, "I have something to say to you."

"Tell me, teacher."

"A certain banker had two clients. One owed him five hundred days' wages, the other fifty. Since neither had the money to pay him, he freely forgave both their debts. Now tell me, which of the two do you think will love him more?"

Simon replied, "I suppose the one who had the deeper debt forgiven."

"You supposed correctly," Jesus said.

He turned to the woman, then said to Simon, "Do you see this woman? When I entered your home, you gave me no water for my feet, but she has washed my feet with her tears and has wiped them with her hair. You didn't give me a welcome kiss, but she has not ceased kissing my feet from the moment I came in. You didn't pour oil on my head, but she poured precious ointment on my feet. Therefore I tell you that her sins, though many, have been forgiven because she loved much. But whoever is forgiven only a little also loves only a little."

Jesus said to her, "Your sins are forgiven."

The other dinner guests began saying to each other, "Who can this be who even forgives sins?"

But Jesus said to the woman, "Your faith has saved you—go in peace."

Soon afterward Jesus traveled to many cities and villages, preaching and announcing the good news, the kingdom of God. The twelve apostles went with him, as well as several women who had been healed of being demonized or various sicknesses. Among them were Mary, called Magdalene, out of whom seven demons had been cast; Joanna, the wife of Herod's servant Chuza; Susanna; and many others, women who kept providing for him from their own resources.

In one place he was greeted by a huge crowd gathered from many towns. He entered a house, which soon became so crowded that he and his disciples couldn't even eat. When his relatives heard about it, they intended to take him home because people were saying, "He has lost his mind."

Then a demonized man, who was both blind and speechless, was brought to Jesus and he healed him, making him both speak and see. This so amazed the gathered crowd that they exclaimed, "Could this be the Son of David?"

But when the Pharisees and teachers of the law from Jerusalem heard it, they said, "He is possessed by Beelzebul, and he casts out demons by the prince of demons."

Knowing their thoughts, Jesus called them to himself and began speaking to them in parables, "How can Satan cast out Satan? A nation that attacks itself cannot survive. And a city or house divided against itself shall not stand. So if Satan has begun to oppose himself and has been divided, he cannot survive, but will be destroyed. Also, if I by Beelzebul cast out demons, by whom then do your sons cast them out? Let them be your judges in this.

"But if I cast out demons by the Spirit of God, then the kingdom of God has come upon you. No one can enter a strong man's house and steal his things, unless he first ties up the strong man. Only then can he plunder his property.

"Whoever is not with me, is against me, and whoever does not gather with me, scatters. This is why I am telling you that every sin and blasphemy will be forgiven, but blasphemy against the Spirit will never be forgiven. Anyone who speaks against the Son of Man will be forgiven, but anyone who speaks against the Holy Spirit will never be forgiven, either in this age or in the age to come. He is guilty of an eternal sin. (He said this because they were saying, "He is demonized.")

"Make a tree good and its fruit will be good; make a tree bad and its fruit will be rotten. A tree is known by its fruit. You children of snakes, how can you speak good things when you are evil?

"The mouth speaks from that which fills the heart. A good person brings good things out of the good treasure of his heart, while an evil person brings evil things out of evil treasure in his heart. I'm telling you that for every careless word that people speak they shall give account on the judgment day. By your words you will be justified, or by your words you will be condemned."

Then some of the learned lawyers and Pharisees replied, "Teacher, we want to see you do a miracle."

In answer Jesus said, "A generation that delights in evil and adultery seeks a sign, but no sign will be given to it except the sign of the prophet Jonah. Just as Jonah himself was in the stomach of the huge fish for three days and three nights, so the Son of Man will be in the depths of the earth three days and three nights.

"The men of Nineveh will stand up with this generation at the judgment and condemn it, because they repented at the preaching of Jonah. Yet someone greater than Jonah is here. The queen of the South will rise up with this generation at the judgment and condemn it, because she came from the ends of the earth to hear the wisdom of Solomon. Yet someone greater than Solomon is here.

"When the demon leaves a person, it passes through desolate areas seeking a place to rest. Not finding one, it says, 'I'll return to the house from which I came.' When it does, it finds the place empty, swept clean, and put in order. Then it departs to gather seven other demons more wicked than itself, and they take up residence there. So the last condition of that person becomes worse than the first. That is the way it will be with this wicked generation."

While he was still speaking to the people and a crowd was seated around him, his mother and brothers arrived. They stood outside and asked to speak with him but were unable to reach him because of the crowd.

Someone told Jesus, "Your mother and brothers are standing outside and want to speak with you."

"Who is my mother," he answered, "and who are my brothers?" He looked about at those sitting around him. Extending his hand toward his disciples he said, "Look at my mother and my brothers! My mother and my brothers are those who hear the word of God and do it. Whoever does the will of my heavenly Father is my brother and sister and mother."

Again that day Jesus began to teach. He went out of the house and sat down beside the sea. Large crowds gathered around, so he boarded a boat and sat in it, while the crowd stood nearby on the shore. He used parables to teach them many things.

"Listen," he said. "A farmer went out to sow his seed. Some seed fell on the pathway where it was trampled, and the birds swooped down and ate it. Other seed fell on rocky places, where there was little soil. It quickly sprouted up. But because it had no root and lacked moisture, it withered away as soon as the sun rose to scorch it. Other seed fell into a thorn patch where the thorns choked out any growth. But some seed fell into good soil and produced a crop—thirty, sixty, and even a hundred times as much as was sown."

Then Jesus called out, "Whoever has ears to hear, let him hear!"

When Jesus was at last alone, the twelve disciples, along with some others, came and asked him, "Why are you speaking in parables to them? And what does this parable mean?"

He answered, "You have been given the privilege of knowing the mysteries of the kingdom of heaven (or of God), but others have not been so privileged. That is why I speak to them in parables, so that though they see, they may not understand, and though they hear, they will not comprehend. Otherwise they may turn and be forgiven.

"The prophecy of Isaiah is fulfilled in them:
'You will indeed hear, but will not comprehend;
* you will indeed see, but not understand at all.*
For the heart of this people has hardened,
* and their ears are full of wax,*
* and their eyes are shut tight—*
* otherwise they might see with their eyes,*
* and hear with their ears,*
* and understand in their heart*
* and be turned back so that I might heal them.'*

"But blessed are your eyes because they see, and your ears because they hear! I tell you the truth, many prophets and righteous men longed to see the things you're seeing, yet did not see them, and to hear the things you're hearing, yet did not hear them."

Then Jesus said to them, "Don't you understand this parable? If not, how will you understand any of the parables? Understand, then, what the parable of the farmer means:

"The seed is the word of God; the farmer is sowing the word. When anyone hears the word of the kingdom and doesn't understand it, then Satan, the evil one, comes immediately to snatch away what was sown in the person's heart, so he cannot believe and be saved. This is the person who received seed on the pathway.

"In a similar way, the one who received seed on the rocky places is the person who hears the word and immediately receives it with delight. But because he isn't well rooted, he continues in his faith only a little while. When hardships or persecution come his way because of the word, immediately he stumbles and falls away.

"The person who received seed among the thorns is the one who hears the word and goes his way. But the worries of this world, the pleasures of life, the seductiveness of wealth, and the passionate desires for material things creep in and choke out the word, making it unfruitful. No fruit ever ripens.

"The person who received seed on the good soil is the one who hears the word with an honest and good heart. He welcomes and understands it, and grips it tightly, and patiently bears much fruit—thirty, sixty, and even a hundred times as much as was sown."

Then he told them another parable: "The kingdom of heaven is like a farmer who planted good seed in his field. But while he slept, an enemy came and planted counterfeit wheat along with the true wheat, then left. When the good wheat began to grow and produce heads of grain, the false wheat grew as well.

"So the farmer's servants said to him, 'Sir, didn't you plant good seed in your field? So where did the false wheat come from?'

"'An enemy did this!' he replied.

"'Would you like us to gather it up?' the servants asked.

"'No,' the farmer answered, 'because you might uproot the true wheat along with the false. Let them grow together until harvest time. Then I will tell the workers, "First collect the false wheat and wrap them in bundles to be burned. But harvest the good wheat and store it in my barn."'"

"Do you take a lamp," Jesus asked them, "and put it under a bowl or a bed? Of course not. No one lights a lamp and then covers it or puts it under a bed. Instead he puts it on a lampstand so people can see where they're going. Nothing is covered that won't be uncovered; nothing is hidden that won't be bathed in light. Whoever has ears to hear, let him hear!"

He also said to them, "Be careful how you listen; pay attention to what you hear. The same measure you use will be used for you—and even more. Whoever has will be given more, and he will have an abundance. But anyone who doesn't have will lose even what he has—or whatever he thinks he has.

"The kingdom of God is like a farmer who plants his seed," Jesus said. "Then the farmer goes to sleep and wakes up, day after day. His seed sprouts and grows, even though he doesn't understand how. All by itself the soil yields a crop—first the shoot, then the ear, then the full head of grain. When the crop is ready, he immediately goes out to harvest it, because the time is right."

He also told them another parable: "What is the kingdom of God like? To what can we compare it? The kingdom of heaven is like a mustard seed that a man planted in his garden. Though it's among the smaller seeds, when it's planted it grows up and becomes a large garden plant. In fact it becomes a tree and sprouts large branches that allow birds to come and roost there and in its shade."

Then he gave them another comparison: "To what can I liken the kingdom of God? The kingdom of heaven is like yeast that a woman poured into three batches of flour until it spread throughout the dough."

Jesus used parables to say all these things to the crowd. With many similar parables he repeated the message so they could understand it. He used nothing but parables to speak to them, to fulfill the words of the prophet:

> "I will speak in parables;
> I will reveal things kept secret
>   since the creation of the world."

In private, however, he explained everything to his disciples.

Then Jesus dismissed the crowds and entered the house, where his disciples asked him, "Please explain to us what the parable of the false wheat means."

He answered, "The farmer who planted the good seed is the Son of Man. The field is the world, and the good seed are the sons of the kingdom. The false wheat stands for the sons of the wicked one, and the enemy who planted them is the devil. The harvest is the end of the age, and the harvesters are the angels. Just as the false wheat was collected and burned, so it will be at the end of this age. The Son of Man will send his angels, and they'll gather up everything in his kingdom that causes people to sin and everyone who does evil. And they'll throw them into the furnace. In that awful place there will be weeping and gnashing of teeth. Then at last God's people will shine as brightly as the sun in their Father's kingdom.

"Whoever has ears to hear, let him hear!"

Once again, the kingdom of heaven is like treasure buried in a field, which a man found and then hid again. In his joy he sells everything he has and buys that field.

"And again, the kingdom of heaven is like a merchant seeking beautiful pearls. When he found one pearl of extremely high value, he sold all he owned and bought it.

"Or yet again, the kingdom of heaven is like a dragnet thrown into the sea, where it caught all kinds of fish. When it was filled and hauled up on shore, workers sat down and sorted all the good fish into baskets. The bad fish they threw away. That is what it will be like at the end of this age.

The angels will go out and remove the wicked from the godly and throw them into the furnace. In that awful place there will be weeping and gnashing of teeth."

Jesus asked them, "Have you understood what I've been saying?"

"Yes, Lord," they answered.

Then he told them, "Every teacher trained for the kingdom of heaven is like the owner of a fine house who brings both new and old things out of his treasure."

That evening when Jesus saw large crowds surrounding him, he ordered his disciples, "Let's cross to the other side of the lake." So his disciples left the crowd and followed him into the boat, taking him just as he was. Then they sailed off, accompanied by several other small vessels.

As they sailed, behold, a violent windstorm swept down on the lake. Waves began breaking over the boat, swamping it and placing them in grave danger. Jesus himself was in the stern, sleeping on a cushion. His disciples woke him. They were crying out, "Master, Master! We're about to die!" "Lord, save us!" "Teacher, don't you care if we die?"

"Why are you so afraid," he said to them, "you who have so little faith?"

Then he got up, rebuked the winds and the raging water, and said to the sea, "Peace! Be still!"

The storm died away, and an intense calm replaced it.

"Where is your faith?" Jesus said to the disciples. "How is it you have no faith?"

The men were astonished and filled with overwhelming awe. "What kind of man is he?" they said to each other. "Who is this, that even wind and sea obey his command?"

They continued sailing down to the country of the Gerasenes, across from Galilee. Immediately after stepping on shore, Jesus was met by two demonized men from the city. They had just come from the tombs and were so fierce that no one dared to travel anywhere near them. One of the men had been demonized a long time and wore no clothes. He lived in the tombs instead of a house. When he saw Jesus in the distance, he cried out, ran to him, and fell down and worshiped him. He shouted, "What do you intend to do to us, Jesus, Son of the Most High God? Did you come here to torture us before the set time? In God's name I beg you, don't torture me!"

This was happening because Jesus had begun to order the demon to come out of the man. For he said to him, "Come out of the man, unclean spirit!"

(The demon had seized him many times, and no one was able to hold him, not even with chains. He had often been restrained with shackles and chains, but he tore apart the chains and broke the shackles in pieces, and no one was able to overpower him. The demon drove him into the desert, and night and day he walked around the mountains and among the tombs, shouting and cutting himself with stones.)

Jesus asked him, "What is your name?"

"My name is Legion," he answered, "because there are many of us here." (Many demons had possessed him.) He began begging Jesus not to order them away from there and into the pit.

Some distance away on the mountainside, a large herd of pigs was feeding. All the demons begged him, "If you cast us out, let us enter the herd of pigs."

"Go," Jesus said at once, giving them permission.

The demons came out of the man and entered the herd of pigs. The whole herd, about two thousand, stampeded down the steep slope and drowned in the lake.

The men who fed the pigs ran away when they saw what happened. They went into the city and the surrounding countryside and reported everything, including the part about the demoniac. Then the whole city came out to meet Jesus and to see for themselves what had happened.

When they met Jesus, they also found the man who had been demonized sitting at Jesus' feet. He was clothed and completely sane—the same one who had been possessed by the Legion—and they were frightened. The men who had seen it happen told them how the demoniac had been cured and about the pigs. Then the people from the Gerasene area asked Jesus to leave, for they were overcome with great fear. So he left.

As Jesus boarded the boat, the man who had been possessed began to beg that he might be allowed to join him. But Jesus would not let him. He sent him away and told him, "Go home to your relatives and tell them what great things the Lord God has done for you and how he had mercy on you."

So the man left and began to report throughout the city and the Decapolis what great things Jesus had done for him. And everyone marveled.

When Jesus crossed the sea and returned to his own town, the people welcomed him, for they had been eagerly awaiting him.

While he was speaking to them, a sizable crowd gathered around him by the shore. A man named Jairus, a synagogue official, came and fell down before Jesus, worshiping him. He begged Jesus to come to his home because his only daughter, who was about twelve years old, was dying.

"My little daughter is at the point of death. Please come and lay your hands on her," he pleaded, "so she'll be healed and live."

Jesus and his disciples got up and left with him, surrounded by a large crowd.

Then a woman who had suffered for twelve years from a hemorrhage heard about Jesus and came up in the throng behind him. This woman had suffered a great deal at the hands of the doctors, yet none of them could cure her. She had spent all she had and still was no better. In fact, she had only become worse. She touched the hem of Jesus' robe because she told herself, "If only I can touch his clothes, I'll be healed." Instantly the bleeding stopped, and she could feel that she had been cured.

At the same moment Jesus sensed that power had gone out from him. He turned around and said, "Who was touching me? Who touched my clothing?"

Everyone denied it. Peter and the disciples who were with him said, "Master, you can see this huge crowd surrounding you—and yet you ask, 'Who touched me?'"

"I know someone touched me," Jesus answered, "because I sensed power leaving me." He began looking at the crowd to see who had done this.

Jesus Raising the Daughter of Jairus

When the woman realized what had happened to her and saw that she couldn't hide, she came to Jesus, frightened and trembling. She fell down before him and told him all the truth. She explained in front of everyone why she had touched him and how she was instantly healed.

Jesus said to her, "Take heart, daughter. Your faith has saved you. Go in peace, and be free from this affliction."

While he was still speaking, someone from the synagogue leader's home arrived and said to the man, "Your daughter has died. Don't bother the teacher anymore."

Jesus heard these remarks, and said to the synagogue leader, "Don't be afraid, just believe. She will be restored to health." He allowed no one to go on with him except Peter, plus James and his brother John, and the girl's father and mother.

When Jesus reached the house, he saw the flute players and the crowd making a commotion. They were weeping and wailing and mourning for her. He entered the house and told them, "Please leave. Why are you making such noise and weeping so? Don't weep, for the girl didn't die but is only sleeping." They knew, however, that she was dead, and they laughed at him.

When he had put them all out, he took the girl's father and mother and those who were with him and entered the room where the child was lying. He took her by the hand and said, "Talitha koum" (which means, "Young girl, get up"). Immediately her spirit returned to her body, and she got up and walked. Then he ordered that she be given something to eat.

Everyone was astonished. Jesus warned them all not to tell others what had happened. Nevertheless, reports about it circulated all over the area.

As Jesus was leaving, two blind men were following him and shouting, "Have mercy on us, Son of David!"

They came closer when he entered another house, and Jesus asked them, "Do you believe I can do this?"

"Yes, Lord!" they replied.

He touched their eyes and said, "Because of your faith, it will be done." Suddenly they could see, and Jesus commanded them, "Don't let anyone know about it." Instead they went out and told everyone in the whole area.

As they were leaving, a demonized man who could not speak was brought to him. When the demon was cast out, the man began talking. The crowds were stunned and said, "We have never seen anything like this in Israel!"

But the Pharisees continued to say, "He is casting out demons through the prince of demons."

Some time afterward there was a Jewish feast, and Jesus went up to Jerusalem. There by the Sheep Gate is a pool (which in the Jewish language is called Bethesda) with five entryways. A crowd of people with various afflictions lay there—the blind, the crippled, and the paralyzed.

One man there had been an invalid for thirty-eight years. When Jesus saw him lying by the pool and knew he had been there a long time, he said to him, "Do you want to get well?"

"Sir," he replied, "I have no one to put me into the pool when the water is stirred. While I am coming, someone else gets there first." (They believed that an angel came down at intervals and energized the waters and whoever stepped in first was healed of his affliction.)

Jesus said to him, "Get up! Pick up your mat and walk." Immediately the man was healed, and he picked up his mat and began walking.

This happened on a Sabbath day, so the Jews said to the man who had been healed, "This is the Sabbath. It's illegal for you to carry the mat."

He answered, "The man who made me well is the one who told me to pick up the mat and walk."

So they asked him, "Who is this man who told you, 'Pick up your mat and walk'?" But he didn't know who it was, since Jesus had left the area because of the large crowd.

Later on Jesus found the man in the temple and said to him, "Now you've been healed. Don't sin anymore so nothing worse happens to you."

The man left and told the Jews it was Jesus who had healed him. And because Jesus was doing such things on the Sabbath, the Jews continued to persecute him and tried to kill him.

Jesus told them, "My Father is continuing to work until now, and so am I."

This made them want even more to kill him. Not only was he breaking the Sabbath, but he also was calling God his own Father, thus making himself equal with God.

Then Jesus said to them, "I tell you the truth, the Son can do nothing by himself. He does only what he sees the Father doing. The Son does whatever the Father does. The Father loves the Son and shows him everything he is doing.

"He will show him even greater things than these, and you will be astonished. Just as the Father raises the dead and makes them alive, so the Son will make alive whomever he wishes. The Father doesn't judge anyone; he has assigned all judgment to the Son that all should honor the Son in the same way they honor the Father. Whoever doesn't honor the Son doesn't honor the Father who sent him.

"I tell you the truth, whoever hears my word and believes the one who sent me has eternal life. He will not be condemned but has already passed out of death into life.

"I tell you the truth, the time is coming—and has already arrived—when dead people will hear the voice of the Son of God and will live. Just as the Father has life in himself, so also he has granted the Son to have life in himself. And he gave him the authority to judge because he is the Son of Man. Don't be surprised at this. Because the time is coming when all who are in their graves will hear his voice and come out—those who have done good, to the resurrection of life, and those who have done evil, to the resurrection of judgment.

"I can do nothing by myself. I judge by what I hear. My judgment is right because I don't seek my will but the will of the Father who sent me.

"If I testify on my own behalf, my testimony is not sufficient. There is another who testifies about me, and I know his witness is true. You yourselves have spoken with John, and he has testified to the truth. Not that I need credentials from any human source, but I say these things so you might be saved. John was the lamp that burned and shone, and you were happy for a while to bask in his light.

"But I have a witness greater even than John. The deeds the Father gave me to do—the very deeds I am doing—testify that the Father has sent me.

"The Father who sent me has himself testified about me. You've never heard his voice nor seen his form—and neither is his word living in you, because you don't believe the one he sent!

"You search the Scriptures because you think you have eternal life in them. Yet these very words testify about me! And you're unwilling to come to me that you might have life.

"I'm not soliciting praise from people, but I know you. I know you don't have the love of God within you. I have come in my Father's name and you refuse to welcome me. If someone else comes in his own name, you'll welcome him! How can you believe when you seek praise from one another but don't seek the praise that comes from the one true God?

"Don't imagine that I will accuse you before the Father. The one who accuses you is Moses, in whom you've put your hope. If you had believed Moses, you would have believed me because he wrote about me. But if you don't believe his writings, how can you believe my words?"

Jesus withdrew from Jerusalem in Judea and entered his boyhood town, along with his disciples. When the Sabbath came, he began to teach them in their synagogue. Many of those who heard him were astonished and asked, "Where did he learn these things?" and "What kind of wisdom is this that enables him to do such miracles? Isn't this the carpenter, the son of a carpenter? Isn't Mary his mother, and aren't James and Joseph and Simon and Jude his brothers? And his sisters—aren't they all here with us?" And they took offense at him.

Then Jesus said to them, "A prophet lacks no honor except in his hometown and among his relatives and in his own home!"

Because of their refusal to believe, he was unable to perform any miracles there, except for a few people who were healed when he laid his hands on them. He was continually amazed at their unbelief.

Then Jesus traveled through all the towns and villages, teaching in their synagogues and continuing to proclaim the good news of the kingdom and healing every sickness and affliction among the people.

When he saw the crowds, he was moved with compassion because they were harassed and helpless, like sheep without a shepherd. He said to his disciples, "The harvest is bountiful, but there are few workers. So then, pray to the Lord of the harvest that he will send out workers into his harvest fields."

He then called his twelve disciples together and gave them power and authority to cast out demons and to heal all kinds of sickness and affliction. Jesus sent them out two by two to proclaim the kingdom of God and to heal the sick.

He gave them this command: "Don't go into Gentile neighborhoods and don't visit any Samaritan city. Go instead to the lost sheep of Israel. As you go, say, 'The kingdom of heaven has arrived!'

"Heal the sick, raise the dead, cure the lepers, cast out demons. Freely you have received, freely give. Don't take anything for the trip except a staff. Don't take along gold or silver or copper in your money belt. Don't take any bread or a bag for provisions. Neither should you take an extra tunic or pair of sandals or staff, but do wear sandals. For the worker deserves his wages.

"Whenever you enter a city or village, find out who in it is worthy. Remain in whatever home you enter until you leave that place. When you enter the home, say a greeting. If the home is indeed worthy, allow your blessing to rest on it. If it isn't worthy, allow your blessing to return to you.

"When you leave a home or a city that refuses to welcome you or hear your message, shake off the dust from under your feet as a testimony against them. I tell you the truth, the day of judgment will be more tolerable for Sodom and Gomorrah than for that city!

"Remember that I am the one who sends you out—as sheep surrounded by wolves. You must be as wise as snakes and as gentle as doves.

"No disciple is greater than his teacher, nor is a slave greater than his master. It's enough for the disciple to become like his teacher and the slave like his master. So if they have called the master of the house 'Beelzebul,' what worse things will they call those in his household!

"Because of this you are not to fear them. There is nothing covered up that won't be uncovered and nothing hidden that won't be revealed. What I'm telling you in the darkness, proclaim in the light; what you hear in whispers, shout on the housetops.

"Don't fear those who can kill the body but are unable to kill the soul. Rather, fear the one who can destroy both soul and body in hell.

"Aren't two sparrows sold for a penny? Yet not one of them will fall to the ground unless your Father allows it. And as for you—why, the very hairs of your head are all numbered. Because this is all true, don't be afraid. You're worth far more than a flock of sparrows!

"Whoever acknowledges me in front of others, I will acknowledge in front of my heavenly Father. But whoever denies me in front of others, I will deny in front of my heavenly Father.

"Don't think that I came to bring peace on earth, but rather a sword. I came to set a man against his father, a daughter against her mother, and a daughter-in-law against her mother-in-law. A man's enemies may be those within his own household.

"Anyone who loves his father or mother more than me is not worthy of me, neither is anyone who loves a son or daughter more than me. And whoever refuses to take his cross and follow me is not worthy of me.

"Whoever finds his life will lose it, and whoever loses his life for my sake will find it.

"Whoever receives you receives me, and whoever receives me receives the one who sent me. Whoever receives a prophet because he is a prophet will receive a prophet's reward, and whoever receives a just person because he is just will receive a just person's reward. And if anyone gives even a cup of cold water to one of these little ones because he is my disciple, I tell you the truth, he will not lose his reward."

When Jesus had finished commissioning his twelve disciples, he left that place to teach and preach in the towns of Galilee.

So they went from village to village announcing the good news and healing everywhere. They preached that people must repent, and they cast out many demons. They also healed many sick people, anointing them with oil.

In those days King Herod the tetrarch heard about all the things Jesus was doing since Jesus was becoming so famous. Herod was perplexed and said, "I beheaded John, so who is doing all these things?"

He wondered about this because some were saying John the Baptist had been raised from the dead. (Others were saying Elijah had appeared, while others claimed that one of the ancient prophets had arisen.) But when Herod heard of it, he said to his servants, "This is John the Baptist, whom I beheaded! He has risen from the dead, and this is why such awesome powers are at work in him." So he began to try to see him.

Herod himself had given the order to arrest John. He had thrown him in prison for the benefit of Herodias, his brother Philip's wife, because he had married her. John had constantly warned Herod, "It's illegal for you to marry your brother's wife." That is why

Herodias had a grudge against him and wanted to kill him, but she had been prevented from doing so. Herod held John in awe, knowing he was a just and holy man. Therefore he kept him safe and enjoyed listening to him though he was exceedingly puzzled. He considered putting John to death, but he refrained from doing so because he feared the people, who believed John to be a prophet.

But the time came when Herod on his birthday held a banquet for his court officials and high-ranking captains and the chief men of Galilee. The daughter of Herodias came in and danced in front of them. She so pleased Herod and his dinner guests that he said to her, "Ask me for anything you want and I'll give it to you." He even swore an oath to her: "No matter what you request, I'll give it to you—even up to half my kingdom!"

She stepped out and asked her mother, "What should I ask for?"

Herodias replied, "The head of John the Baptist."

So her daughter returned quickly to the king and said, "I want you to give me at once the head of John the Baptist on a platter."

The king was very unhappy. But because of his promise and those eating with him, he would not refuse her request. He ordered an executioner to bring him John's head. So the man left and beheaded

John in prison. He brought the head back on a platter and presented it to the young woman, who gave it to her mother.

When John's disciples heard what had happened, they came and took his body and buried it in a tomb. Then they went to tell Jesus. When he heard what had happened, he left the place he had been.

When the apostles returned, they reported to Jesus everything they had done and taught. Then he said to them, "Come away by yourselves to a quiet spot and rest for a while."

Many people were coming and going, and the disciples didn't even have time to eat. So he took them and left in the boat for the other side of the Sea of Galilee (or Sea of Tiberias) to go to a quiet spot near the city of Bethsaida.

Somehow the crowds learned of it and saw them leaving, and many recognized him. So on foot they hurried in that direction, coming from all the towns. (They followed him because they saw the miracles he performed on the sick.) Arriving first, they came as one group toward Jesus.

When he stepped on shore, he saw the huge crowd. He was moved with compassion toward them because they were like sheep without a shepherd. He welcomed them and began to teach them many things. He talked to them about the kingdom of God and healed those who needed it.

Late in the day Jesus went up the mountain and sat down there with his disciples. (Now the Passover, the Jewish feast, was approaching.) When Jesus looked up and saw the large crowd coming his way, he said to Philip, "Where can we buy bread so these people may eat?" He said this only to test him, because he already knew what he was going to do.

Philip answered, "Two hundred days' wages wouldn't buy enough bread for each of them to have even a little."

The disciple Andrew (Simon's brother) said to him, "A young boy here has five barley loaves and two small fish. But what good will that do for such a large crowd?"

The twelve then said to him, "This place is remote and it's already late. Send the crowds away so they can go into the villages and the surrounding area to find some place to stay and eat."

"They don't need to go away," Jesus replied. "You give them something to eat."

They answered, "Do you want us to go and buy two hundred days' wages worth of bread and give them that to eat?"

"How many loaves do you have?" he replied. "Go and find out."

Once they found out, they said to him, "We have only five loaves and two fish—unless we indeed go and buy food for all this crowd!"

But Jesus said, "Bring the food here to me."

Then he said to his disciples, "Have the people sit down to eat, in groups of fifty." The place was a grassy area, and the disciples had everyone sit on the grass in groups of fifty and a hundred. Then Jesus took the five loaves and two fish, looked up to heaven, and blessed them. Once he had given thanks, he broke the loaves and gave them to the disciples to distribute to the crowd. He did the same thing with the two small fish, giving them as much as they wanted. All of them ate until they were satisfied.

When they were all full, he said to his disciples, "Gather up the leftover pieces; make sure you don't lose anything." So they gathered them up and filled twelve baskets with pieces from the five barley loaves and the fish left over after everyone finished eating. About five thousand men had eaten that day, besides women and children.

When the people saw the miracle Jesus did, they said, "Without question this is the prophet who was to come into the world."

Jesus perceived that they were ready to come and make him king by force. So at once he insisted that his disciples board the boat and sail to the other side to Bethsaida, while he dismissed the crowds.

After sending the people away, he again went up the mountain by himself to pray.

As evening fell his disciples had gone down to the sea, boarded the boat, and started to sail across to Capernaum. By now it was dark and Jesus had not yet joined them. Then a strong wind began blowing, and the sea became rough.

Jesus, alone on the land, saw them straining at their oars. The boat was now in the middle of the sea and was being pounded by waves whipped up by wind, which was blowing against them. In the fourth watch of the night, after they had rowed between three and four miles, Jesus walked toward them on the sea.

He intended to come beside them, but when the disciples saw him walking on the sea and getting closer to the boat, they were frightened and said, "It's a ghost!" They cried out in fear, because they all saw him and were terrified.

"Take courage!" Jesus called out to them at once. "It is I! Don't be afraid."

Then Peter answered, "Lord, if it really is you, tell me to join you on the water."

Jesus Walking on the Sea

"Come," Jesus said.

Peter then climbed out of the boat and walked on the water toward Jesus. But when he saw the howling wind, he was frightened. He began to sink. "Lord, save me!" he shouted.

Jesus quickly extended his hand and caught him. "You have so little faith," he said to Peter. "What made you doubt?"

Then they willingly received him in the boat, and the wind stopped after they climbed into the boat. All of them were confounded and filled with awe because they hadn't understood about the loaves of bread—their hearts were unreceptive. But they worshiped him, saying, "You are truly the Son of God."

Just then they arrived at the shore where they were heading, in the region of Gennesaret, and they got out of the boat. People there recognized Jesus at once. They ran throughout the countryside and brought those who were ill, carrying them on mats to wherever they heard he was.

Every place Jesus went—whether a village, a town, or the countryside—they kept laying the sick in the marketplaces and begging to be allowed just to touch the edge of his garment. And everyone who touched it was restored to health.

THE THIRD YEAR
OF MINISTRY

April AD 31 — March AD 32

The next day the people who remained on the other side of the sea realized that no other boat had been there except the one Jesus' disciples had entered. (Jesus hadn't entered their boat; they had gone off by themselves.) Then other boats from Tiberias landed close to where they had eaten the bread after Jesus gave thanks. When the people saw that neither Jesus nor his disciples were there, they climbed aboard the boats and sailed to Capernaum, looking for Jesus.

When they found him on the other side of the sea, they said to him, "Rabbi, when did you come here?"

Jesus answered, "I tell you the truth, you don't look for me because you saw some miracles, but because you filled your stomachs with bread. Don't work for food that spoils, but for the lasting food that gives eternal life. The Son of Man can give you such food, because God the Father has placed his seal of approval on him."

Then they asked him, "What sort of thing should we be doing to satisfy God's requirements?"

Jesus answered, "The work God requires is this: believe in the one he sent."

"What miracle are you doing," they asked, "to convince us we should believe you? What demonstration do you offer? Our ancestors ate manna in the desert. As the Scripture says, 'he gave them heavenly bread to eat.'"

Jesus replied, "I tell you the truth, Moses didn't give you the heavenly bread. Rather, it is my Father who gives you the true heavenly bread. God's bread comes down out of heaven and gives life to the world."

"Then sir," they said, "give us this bread from now on!"

Jesus said to them, "I am the bread of life. The one who comes to me will never grow hungry, and the one who believes in me will never get thirsty. But I'm telling you that though you've seen me, you don't believe!

"Everyone the Father gives to me will surely come to me. And the one who comes to me I will never send away.

"I have come down from heaven to do the will of the one who sent me, not to do my own will. And the will of the Father who sent me is this: that I should not lose even one of all those he has given me—indeed, I will raise them all up at the last day. The will of the one who sent me is this: that everyone who sees the Son and believes in him should have eternal life. And I will raise them up at the last day."

The Jews began to grumble about him because he said, "I am the bread which came down from heaven." They kept saying, "Isn't he Jesus, the son of Joseph? Don't we know his father and mother? Then how can he say 'I have come down from heaven'?"

"Stop your grumbling," Jesus said. "No one can come to me unless the Father who sent me draws him—and I will raise him up at the last day.

"One of the prophets wrote, 'God will teach everyone.' Everyone who has listened to and learned from the Father comes to me. Not that anyone has seen the Father, except the one who has come from God. He has seen the Father.

"I tell you the truth, the one who believes in me has eternal life. I am the bread of life. Your ancestors in the desert ate the manna and yet they died. But this is the bread that comes down from heaven, which anyone may eat and not die.

"I am the living bread that came down from heaven. If anyone eats this bread, he will live forever. The bread I offer is my body, which I will give for the life of the world."

Then the Jews began to argue with one another. "How can he give us his body to eat?" they demanded.

"I tell you the truth," he said, "unless you eat the body of the Son of Man and drink his blood, you will not have life. Whoever eats my body and drinks my blood has eternal life, and I will raise him up at the last day.

"My body is true food and my blood is true drink. Whoever eats my body and drinks my blood remains in me, and I in him. As the living Father sent me—and I live through the Father—so the one who eats my body will live through me. This is the bread that came down from heaven. This bread is very different from the manna your ancestors ate, because they died. Whoever eats this bread will live forever."

He said these things while he was teaching in the synagogue in Capernaum. When many of his disciples heard him, they said, "This is a difficult message. Who can accept it?"

Jesus sensed that his disciples were grumbling about this and said to them, "Does this offend you? Then what should happen if you were to see the Son of Man ascending to where he was before? It is the Spirit who gives life; the mere body accomplishes nothing. My words are both spirit and life. But some of you don't believe!"

Jesus knew from the very first who did not believe and even who would betray him. He said, "This is why I said to you that no one can come to me unless my Father permits."

From that time on many of his disciples left and no longer followed him. Jesus said to the twelve, "Do you also want to leave?"

Simon Peter answered, "Lord, to whom can we go? You have words of eternal life! We have come to believe and are convinced that you are the holy one of God."

Jesus replied, "Didn't I choose the twelve of you? And yet one of you is a devil!" (He was speaking of Judas, the son of Simon Iscariot. Though he was one of the twelve, he would one day betray him.)

Jesus continued his traveling ministry around Galilee. He refused to go to Judea because the Jews were seeking to kill him.

One day some Pharisees and teachers of the law from Jerusalem surrounded him. When they saw the disciples eating with "unclean" hands (that is, ceremonially unwashed), they began criticizing them. (The

Pharisees and the rest of the Jews don't eat until they ceremonially wash their hands—a tradition handed down from their ancestors. When they come from the marketplace, they don't eat until they ceremonially wash themselves. They also observe many other ancient traditions, such as the washing of cups and pots and bronze utensils.)

So the Pharisees and the teachers of the law asked him, "Why do your disciples disregard the tradition of our ancestors? See, they do not wash their hands before eating."

"You hypocrites!" Jesus answered. "Isaiah accurately prophesied about you when he wrote:

> 'This people honors me with their lips,
>   but their heart is far from me.
> They worship me in vain
>   and teach human regulations
>   as if they were divine commands.'

"You disregard the commands of God and instead obey human traditions, such as the washing of pots and cups. And you do many other things just like that.

"Is it right for you to ignore the commands of God in order to obey your tradition? Moses proclaimed God's commands: 'Honor your father and mother,' and, 'Whoever slanders his father or mother must be put to death.' But you say that if anyone tells his father or mother, 'Anything I have that might help you is Corban, that it has been given to God'—so that the person ignores his parents—you allow him to neglect the honoring of his father and mother. In this way you use your tradition to set aside the commandment of God, and you make his word mean nothing. You're doing many other things just like that."

When he had called everyone together, he said, "Listen to me and understand, all of you. What goes into a person's mouth can never make him unclean. What makes him unclean are the words that come out of his mouth. If anyone has ears to hear, let him hear."

Then his disciples approached him and said, "Did you know the Pharisees were offended by that statement?"

"Every plant my heavenly Father did not plant will be pulled up by the roots," he answered. "Leave them alone; they are blind leaders leading blind people— and if the blind lead the blind, all of them will fall into a pit together."

After he entered a house away from the crowd, his disciples asked him about the parable. "Please explain it to us," Peter said.

Jesus answered, "Do you, too, still fail to understand? Don't you see that whatever enters the mouth from outside cannot possibly make a person ceremonially unclean? It doesn't enter his heart, but only his body, and is later eliminated." (By saying this he made all foods ceremonially clean.)

"What comes out of a person's mouth shows what is in his heart," Jesus said. "Those things make him unclean. Evil things come from within, from the heart—murder, adultery, sexual sins, theft, false testifying, blasphemy, envy, malicious deeds, deceit, promiscuity, lust, conceit, foolishness—all these corrupt things come from within. These make a person unclean. But eating with ceremonially unwashed hands does not make anyone unclean."

Then Jesus left that place to travel to the vicinity of Tyre and Sidon. He entered a house and wanted to keep it a secret, but word got out. A Canaanite woman from that area (she was a Gentile from Syrian Phoenicia) heard he was there. She came and fell at his feet and pleaded with him: "Take pity on me, Lord, Son of David! My daughter is demonized." She begged him to cast the demon out of her daughter.

Jesus, however, said not a single word in reply. And his disciples came and urged him, "Send her away. She keeps calling after us."

Then Jesus said, "I was not sent to anyone except the lost sheep of Israel."

But the woman worshiped him. "Lord, help me!" she said.

"The children must first be fed," Jesus replied. "It isn't right to take the children's bread and throw it to the dogs."

"Yes, Lord!" she answered. "But even the dogs eat the children's crumbs that fall from the table."

Jesus replied, "O woman, your faith is great! Because of your reply, your request is granted. Go on home. The demon has left your daughter."

From that very moment her daughter was healed. When the woman returned home, she found her daughter lying on the bed and the demon gone.

Then Jesus left the vicinity of Tyre and Sidon and went down to the Sea of Galilee and into the area of the Decapolis. Some people brought a deaf man with a speech impediment to him and begged him to lay his hand on the man.

Jesus took the man away from the crowd, put his fingers in his ears, spat, and touched his tongue. Then he looked up to heaven and sighed, and said to him, "Ephphatha" (which means, "Open up!"). Immediately the man could hear and speak clearly.

Jesus strictly warned the people not to tell anyone, but the more he warned them the more they kept announcing it. They were amazed and said, "He does everything well! He causes even deaf people to hear and mute people to speak."

Then Jesus traveled along the Sea of Galilee, went up on a mountain, and sat down. Enormous crowds came to him there, bringing with them the lame, the blind, the mute, the maimed, and many others. They hurried to place these people at Jesus' feet, and he healed them all. The crowds were astounded to see the mute speaking, the maimed healed, the lame walking, and the blind seeing. So they praised the God of Israel.

One day there was a large crowd who had nothing to eat. Jesus called his disciples together and said to them, "I am greatly concerned for these people because they have been with me here for three days and have nothing to eat. I refuse to send them home on empty stomachs because they might collapse on the way. Some of them have come a long way."

His disciples answered, "Where can we find enough bread out here in this desolate place to feed such a huge crowd?"

So Jesus asked them, "How many loaves of bread do you have?"

They replied, "Seven, and a few little fish."

Then Jesus ordered the crowd to sit on the ground. After he took the seven loaves and the fish, he gave thanks and broke them in pieces and handed them to his disciples to serve the people. They all ate until they were full. Then they collected seven baskets full of leftovers. There were about four thousand men present, besides women and children.

Then he dismissed the crowd and immediately boarded the boat with his disciples. They were heading for the district of Dalmanutha in the neighborhood of Magadan. The Pharisees and Sadducees came out to meet him and began to argue with him, demanding that he show them a miracle from heaven. They did this to test him.

He said to them, "In the evening you say, 'It will be good weather' when the sky is red. And in the morning you say, 'A storm is brewing' when the sky is red and menacing. [You hypocrites!] You know how to forecast the weather, but somehow you cannot recognize the signs of the times!"

Sighing deeply he said, "Why does this generation demand a sign? Only a wicked and adulterous generation demands a sign. But I tell you the truth, it will get no sign except for the sign of the prophet Jonah." With that he left them, boarded the boat, and once more sailed toward the opposite shore.

The disciples had forgotten to take bread along, except for a single loaf. When they reached the opposite shore, Jesus warned them, "Watch out for the yeast of the Pharisees and the Sadducees and of Herod."

They began asking each other, "Is he saying this because we forgot to take along bread?"

Jesus knew what they were discussing and said, "Why do you ask each other about forgetting to bring bread, you of little faith? Don't you understand yet? Do you still not comprehend? Are your minds still so dense? You have eyes—don't you see? You have ears—don't you hear? And don't you remember? When I broke the five loaves for the crowd of five thousand, how many baskets full of leftovers did you gather?"

They answered, "Twelve."

"And when I broke the seven loaves for the crowd of four thousand, how many baskets full of leftovers did you gather?"

"Seven," they replied.

"So how can you still fail to understand? Why can't you see that I wasn't talking about bread when I warned you about the yeast of the Pharisees and Sadducees?"

Then they finally understood that he hadn't warned them about the yeast of bread but about the teaching of the Pharisees and the Sadducees.

When he arrived in Bethsaida, some men brought a blind man to him and begged him to touch the man. He took the blind man by the hand and led him out of the village. Then he wiped some spit on his eyes, laid his hands on him, and asked if he saw anything.

The man looked up and said, "I see people! They look like walking trees."

When Jesus laid his hands on the man's eyes again and had him look up, his sight was restored and he saw everyone clearly. Then Jesus sent him home, saying, "Don't go into the village."

The Jewish Feast of Tabernacles was approaching, so Jesus' brothers said to him, "Leave here and go to Judea, so your disciples can see what you're doing. Nobody acts in secret when he wants to be known publicly. If you're really doing these things, show yourself to the world." (Not even his brothers believed in him.)

"My time has not yet arrived," Jesus replied, "but your time is always ready! The world cannot hate you, but it hates me because I say that what it does is evil. Go on up to the feast; I am not yet going because my time hasn't fully arrived."

So he stayed in Galilee. Only after his brothers had gone did he also leave for the feast. He didn't go publicly, however, but in secret.

The Jews were looking for Jesus at the Feast of Tabernacles. "Where is that man?" they kept asking. There was considerable discussion about him among the people. Some were saying, "He's a good man." Others said, "No, he isn't; he's deceiving the people." But nobody spoke openly about him because they were afraid of the Jews.

At the midpoint of the feast, Jesus went into the temple and began to teach. The Jews were astonished and said, "How does this man know so much, since he has never been to school?"

Jesus answered, "My teaching is not my own. It comes from the one who sent me. If anyone wants to do God's will, he will know whether this teaching is from him or whether I am speaking on my own.

"Anyone who speaks on his own seeks his own glory. But the one who seeks the glory of the one who sent him is true and does only what is right. Didn't Moses give you the law? Yet none of you keeps the law. Why do you want to kill me?"

"You're demonized!" the people answered. "Who wants to kill you?"

Jesus replied, "I did one miracle, and you all are astonished. Moses gave you the rite of circumcision—not that he originated it, since it was handed down from the patriarchs—and you circumcise a male on the Sabbath. If a male is circumcised on the Sabbath so the law of Moses should not be broken, why are you angry with me for healing a man's whole body on the Sabbath? Don't judge by the way things look; judge rightly."

Some people in Jerusalem were saying, "Isn't he the one they wanted to kill? Yet he is speaking in public and they don't even notice! Do you think our rulers have concluded that he really is the Messiah? But that makes no sense—we know this man and where he's from. No one will know where the Messiah comes from when he appears."

At that time Jesus began to teach in the temple, speaking in a loud voice: "So you think you know me and where I'm from! Yet I haven't come on my own authority. The one who is true sent me. And you don't know him! I do know him, however, because I came from him. He sent me."

They kept looking for a way to arrest him. Yet nobody laid a hand on him because his time had not yet arrived. Many people in the crowd believed in him. They said, "When the Messiah comes, will he do any greater miracles than what this man has done?"

When the Pharisees heard what the people were saying about Jesus, they and the chief priests sent officers to arrest him. Jesus said to them, "I am with you for only a little while longer, then I will return to the one who sent me.

"You will look for me but won't be able to find me. Where I am going you cannot come."

Then the Jews said to each other, "Where does he intend to go so we won't be able to find him? Do you think he'll go to those who are living among the Greeks in order to teach the Greeks? What does he mean when he says, 'You will look for me but won't be able to find me,' and 'Where I am going you cannot come'?"

On the last day of the feast, known as the "Great Day," Jesus stood and said in a loud voice, "If anyone is thirsty, let him come to me and drink! Whoever puts his trust in me, out of the depths of his being will flow rivers of living water, even as the Scripture has said."

(He said this about the Holy Spirit, who in the future would be given to everyone who believed. At this time the Holy Spirit had not yet come, since Jesus was not yet glorified.)

When many of the people heard what Jesus taught, they said, "Without question this is the prophet." Others said, "He is the Messiah!" Still others said, "He can't be. The Messiah won't come from Galilee! Doesn't Scripture say that the Messiah will be a descendant of David and will come from Bethlehem, David's own village?"

So the people were divided in their opinion of him. Some wanted to seize him, yet nobody laid a hand on him. The officers then returned to the chief priests and Pharisees, who asked their men, "Why didn't you bring him to us?"

"Nobody ever spoke like this Man does!" the officers replied.

"Have you, too, been deceived?" the Pharisees responded. "Have any of the authorities believed in him? Have any of the Pharisees? This mob that doesn't know the law at all is cursed!"

Nicodemus, the man who visited Jesus at night, was a member of the ruling council. He said to them, "Does our law judge a man before first giving him a hearing to know what he is doing?"

They answered, "You aren't from Galilee, too, are you? Look into it—no prophet has ever come from Galilee."

Then everyone went home, while Jesus went to the Mount of Olives.

At dawn Jesus came back to the temple. All the people gathered around, so he sat down and began to teach them.

Then the teachers of the law and the Pharisees brought to him a woman who had been caught in adultery. They forced her to stand before the crowd. Then they said to Jesus, "Teacher, this woman was caught in adultery, in the very act. In the law Moses commanded us to stone such a person. But what do you say?" The only reason they said this was to trap him, to find some way of accusing him.

Jesus bent down and began to write something in the dirt with his finger. When they kept questioning him, he rose up and said, "Whoever of you has never sinned, throw the first stone at her." He bent down again and continued writing in the dirt.

[His words pricked their consciences.] One by one they began to leave the area, beginning with the oldest. When they had all gone, Jesus was left alone with the woman, who was still standing there.

When Jesus stood up and saw no one except the woman, he said to her, "Woman, where are your accusers? Didn't anyone stay to condemn you?"

"No one, sir," she replied.

"Then I don't condemn you, either. Go on your way, and stop sinning."

Again Jesus taught them all, saying, "I am the light of the world. Whoever follows me will not walk around in the dark; instead, he'll have the light of life."

Jesus and the Woman Taken in Adultery

The Pharisees said to him, "You're testifying about yourself, so your testimony isn't valid."

Jesus answered, "Although I am testifying about myself, my testimony is valid. I know where I came from and where I am going, but you know neither where I came from nor where I am going. You judge by human standards.

"On the other hand, I am not judging anyone. Still, if I do judge, my judgment is valid, because I'm not alone. The Father who sent me is with me. Furthermore, your law says that the testimony of two people is valid. I am testifying about myself, and the Father who sent me is doing likewise."

"Where is your Father?" they asked.

"You don't know me or my Father," Jesus answered. "If you had known me, you would have known my Father also." Jesus said these things as he was teaching in the temple treasury. Yet nobody placed him under arrest because his time had not yet arrived.

Once more he spoke to them: "I am going away and you will search for me, and you will die in your sin. Where I am going you cannot come."

So the Jews said, "Will he kill himself, since he says, 'Where I am going you cannot come'?"

Jesus said to them, "You are from beneath; I am from above. You are from this world; I am not from this world.

"That is why I told you that you will die in your sins. If you don't believe that I am, you will die in your sins."

"Who are you?" the Jews asked.

"I am exactly what I have been telling you all along," Jesus answered. "I have a great many things to say to you and to judge about you. But the one who sent me is faithful, and the things I heard from him are what I am saying to the world."

They didn't understand that he was speaking to them about the Father. So Jesus said to them, "After you have lifted up the Son of Man, then you will know that I am, and that I do nothing on my own. Rather, I say only what my Father instructed me to say. The one who sent me is with me. The Father did not abandon me, because I always do what pleases him."

Many people believed in him because of what he said. Then Jesus said to those who believed, "If you continue in my word you will indeed be my disciples. You will know the truth, and the truth will set you free."

"We are the descendants of Abraham," they said, "and have never been anyone's slaves. How can you say we will be set free?"

"I tell you the truth," Jesus replied, "everyone who practices sin is a slave to that sin. The slave doesn't live in the home forever, but the son does. That is why if the Son sets you free, you will truly be free.

"I know you are descendants of Abraham. But you want to kill me because you refuse to accept what I am saying. I am talking about the things I have seen in my Father's presence. In the same way, you're doing what you have seen in your father's presence."

"Abraham is our father," they said.

"If you were children of Abraham," Jesus answered, "you would do the things Abraham did. Instead you want to kill me—someone who has told you the truth, straight from God. Abraham did nothing like this! You're following the example of your father."

"We are not illegitimate!" they said. "We have only one Father—God himself."

"If God were really your father," Jesus answered, "you would have loved me, since I came from God. I did not come on my own. He sent me.

"Why is it you can't understand what I am saying? It's because you can't accept my message. You're from your father, the devil, and you want to act out your father's desires. He was a murderer from the beginning and he rejects the truth because truth has no place in him. When he lies, he speaks what is natural to him, because he's a liar and the father of lies.

"It's because I tell the truth that you don't believe me! Who of you can show that I've committed any sin? So if I'm telling the truth, why don't you believe me? Anyone who belongs to God listens to God's words. This is the very reason you don't listen to them: you do not belong to God."

"Aren't we right," the Jews answered, "in saying that you're a Samaritan and demonized?"

Jesus replied, "I am not demonized. Instead I am honoring my Father, and you are dishonoring me. Yet I don't seek after my own glory.

"There is one who is both seeking it and making judgments. I tell you the truth, if anyone will act on what I say, he will never experience death."

"Now we know you're demonized!" the Jews said. "Abraham died, as did the prophets. Yet you say, 'If anyone will act on what I say, he will never experience death.' Are you greater than our forefather Abraham, who died? The prophets died, too. Just who do you think you are?"

Jesus answered, "It means nothing if I should glorify myself. It is my Father who glorifies me—the one you claim as your God, yet he is unknown to you! But I know him. If I were to say I don't know him, I would be a liar like you. But I do know him, and I keep his word. Your forefather Abraham had great joy to think he would see my day. And when he did see it he was glad."

"You aren't yet fifty years old," the Jews replied. "How could you have seen Abraham?"

"I tell you the truth," Jesus said, "Before Abraham existed, I AM."

At this they picked up stones to throw at him. But Jesus hid himself and left the temple, going on his way.

As Jesus was walking along he saw a man who had been born blind. His disciples asked him, "Rabbi, whose sins caused this, this man's or his parents?"

"It was neither the sins of this man nor of his parents," Jesus answered. "Rather, it happened so that the works of God might be seen. While it is still day, I must do what the Father sent me to do. The night is coming, when no one can work. As long as I remain in the world, I am the light of the world."

After he said these things, he spat on the ground and made some mud and applied it to the blind man's eyes. "Go wash in the Pool of Siloam," he told the man. (Siloam means "sent.") The man left and washed, then came back seeing.

His neighbors and those who had known him when he was blind said, "Isn't this the man who was sitting and begging?"

Some said, "Yes, it is," but others said, "He just looks like him."

The man himself said, "I'm the one!"

"How did you receive your sight?" they asked him.

He answered, "A man named Jesus made some mud, put it on my eyes, and told me, 'Go wash in the Pool of Siloam.' So I left, and washed, and then I could see."

"Where is he?" they demanded.

"I don't know," he replied.

Then they brought to the Pharisees the man who had been blind. Since Jesus had made the mud and given the man his sight on the Sabbath, the Pharisees began to ask him again how he had received his sight.

"He put mud on my eyes, I washed, and now I see," he said.

Some of the Pharisees responded, "That man cannot be from God because he doesn't keep the Sabbath!" Others said, "How can a sinner do miracles?" So they were divided.

They asked the blind man again, "What do you say about him, since he gave you your sight?"

"He is a prophet," the man replied.

The Jews would not believe that he had been blind and had been given sight until they called his parents and asked them, "Is this your son, whom you say was born blind? If so, then how is it that he can now see?"

"We know this is our son," his parents answered, "and we know he was born blind. But we don't know how he is able to see now, or who gave him his sight. He's an adult; why don't you ask him? He can speak for himself." (His parents said this because they were afraid of the Jews, who had already agreed that anyone acknowledging Jesus as the Messiah would be kicked out of the synagogue. That is why the man's parents said, "He's an adult; why don't you ask him?")

Once more the Jews called the man who had been blind. They said to him, "Give praise to God. We know this man is a sinner."

"I don't know whether he's a sinner or not," the man answered. "But I do know this: I was blind, but now I can see."

"What did he do to you?" they asked him. "How did he give you your sight?"

"I already told you and you didn't listen. Why do you want to hear it again? Do you want to become his disciples, too?"

At this, they ridiculed him and said, "You're his disciple. We're disciples of Moses. We know God has spoken to Moses, but we don't even know where this man comes from."

"That's truly remarkable," the man replied. "You don't know where he comes from, yet he gave me my sight. We know God refuses to hear sinners, but he gladly hears those who worship him and do his will. Never before in history has it been reported that someone born blind was given sight. If this were not from God, he couldn't do anything."

"You were born a wretched sinner!" they said to him. "Do you dare to teach us?" Then they kicked him out.

Jesus heard they had kicked him out, and when he found the man he said to him, "Do you believe in the Son of God?"

"Who is he, sir," the man answered, "so I might believe in him?"

"You are looking at him," Jesus replied. "He is speaking with you now."

"Lord," the man said, "I believe." And he worshiped him.

Then Jesus said, "I came into this world to pass judgment, that the blind may see and those who see might be blinded."

Some Pharisees who happened to be there heard this and said, "Are we blind, too?"

"If you were blind," Jesus answered, "you wouldn't be guilty of a sin. But since you say, 'We see,' your sin is self-evident.

"I tell you the truth, anyone who enters the sheepfold by some way other than the door is a thief and a robber. But the one who uses the door to enter is the shepherd of the sheep. The gatekeeper opens the door for him. The sheep hear his voice, and he calls them by name and leads them out.

"When all the sheep are out he walks in front of them, and the sheep follow him because they know his voice. They refuse to follow a stranger, but they will follow him. They don't recognize the voice of strangers."

Jesus directed this parable at them, but they didn't understand what he was trying to tell them. So he spoke to them again: "I tell you the truth, I am the door for the sheep. All those who preceded me were thieves and robbers, and the sheep refused to listen to them. I am the door. Anyone who enters through me will be saved and will go in and out and find pasture. The thief comes only to steal and kill and destroy, but I came to give them life—and life more abundantly.

"I am the good shepherd. The good shepherd gives up his life for the sheep. But the hired hand is not their shepherd and doesn't own them. He sees a wolf coming, abandons the sheep, and runs away. Then the wolf attacks the flock and scatters it. The hired hand runs away because he is a hired hand and doesn't care about the sheep.

"I am the good shepherd. I know those who belong to me, and they know me, just as the Father knows me, and I know him. I am giving up my life for the sheep. I also have other sheep who do not belong to this fold.

I must also bring them, and they will hear my voice. At that time there will be one flock and one shepherd.

"Because I am giving up my life, the Father loves me. I give it up so I might claim it again. No one takes it away from me. I am giving it up of my own free will. I have the authority to give it up, and I have the authority to claim it again. I received this command from my Father."

These words caused a new dispute among the Jews.

Many of them said, "He has a demon and is raving mad. Why listen to him?"

But others said, "These are not the words of a demonized man. Can a demon open the eyes of the blind?"

Then came the Feast of Dedication in Jerusalem. It was winter, and Jesus was walking around in the temple, in the Colonnade of Solomon. The Jews soon gathered around him and asked, "How long are you going to keep us in suspense? If you're the Messiah, tell us plainly."

Jesus answered, "I already told you, and you don't believe. The things I'm doing in the name of my Father testify to my identity. You don't believe because you aren't my sheep.

"I've already told you that my sheep hear my voice. I know them and they follow me. I give them eternal life and they will never die. Neither will anyone take them away from me. My Father, who gave them to me, is greater than all, and no one can take them away from my Father. I and the Father are one."

Because of this the Jews once more began picking up stones to throw at him.

"I've done many great miracles from the Father," Jesus said. "For which of them do you intend to stone me?"

"We aren't stoning you for any of them," the Jews answered, "but because you have blasphemed. You, a mere man, are claiming to be God!"

Jesus replied, "Is it not written in your own law, 'I said, you are gods'? This word 'gods' describes those who received God's word—and Scripture cannot be broken. So why do you charge me with blasphemy for saying I am the Son of God, when the Father set me apart and sent me into the world? Don't believe me if I'm not doing what my Father does. But if I am doing it, then even though you don't believe me, believe the things I'm doing. Then you will understand and believe that the Father is in me and I am in him."

Again they tried to arrest him, but he escaped their grasp.

Then he left once more for the other side of the Jordan, where John did his baptizing. Jesus stayed there, and many people came to visit him. "John, of course, performed no miracles," they said, "but everything John said about this man is true." And many people in that place believed in him.

THE FOURTH YEAR
OF MINISTRY

April AD 32 — March AD 33

Jesus and his disciples left there and went to the villages of Caesarea Philippi. During the trip he was praying by himself. The disciples were with him, and he asked them, "Who do people say that I, the Son of Man, am?"

"Some say John the Baptist," they answered. "Others say Elijah, and still others say Jeremiah, or that some ancient prophet has reappeared."

"But you," he said to them—"Who do you say I am?"

Simon Peter answered, "You are the Messiah, the Son of the living God."

"Blessed are you, Simon son of Jonah!" Jesus said. "Flesh and blood did not reveal this to you, but my

Father in heaven. And I tell you that you are Peter, and on this rock I will build my church. All the gates of hell will not overcome it. I will give you the keys to the kingdom of heaven. Whatever you bind on earth will have been bound in heaven, and whatever you release on earth will have been released in heaven."

At that time he strictly warned his disciples to tell no one that he was the Messiah.

From that time on Jesus began to tell his disciples that he must travel to Jerusalem. "The Son of Man must suffer many things and be rejected by the elders and chief priests and teachers of the law. He must be killed and on the third day be raised again." He said all this publicly.

But Peter took him aside and rebuked him to his face. "No, Lord!" he said. "This will never happen to you."

Turning around, Jesus looked at all the disciples, then said to Peter, "Get behind me, Satan! You're a stumbling block in my way. You don't have in mind the things of God, but the things of men."

Then Jesus called everyone to join his disciples, and he said to them all, "If anyone chooses to come after me, he must put his own desires to one side, pick up his cross every day, and follow me. Whoever intends to save his life will lose it. But whoever loses

his life for my sake and for that of the good news
will save it—he will find it.

"What good is it if someone obtains the whole
world but destroys himself or loses his soul? What can
a man give in exchange for his soul?

"If anyone is ashamed of me and my words in this
adulterous and sinful generation, the Son of Man will
be ashamed of him when he comes in his glory and
that of the Father and the holy angels. At that time he
will reward each person according to what he has done.

"I tell you the truth, some of you standing here will
not die before you see the Son of Man coming in his
kingdom—the kingdom of God coming with power."

Six days later Jesus took Peter and James and his
brother John up on a high mountain so they could
pray by themselves. As he was praying, his appearance
changed and he was transformed before their eyes. His
face grew as bright as the sun, and his clothes began to
shine a brilliant white, like snow, whiter than any washing could bleach them—a radiant white, like light itself.

Suddenly two men—Moses and Elijah—appeared
before them. They also were shining, and they talked
about his coming departure which would occur
in Jerusalem. Peter and his companions had been
nodding off to sleep, but now were wide awake as they
saw his glory and the two men standing with him.

As the men began to leave him, Peter said to Jesus, "Lord, it's good for us to be here. If you want us to, we could make three shelters—one for you, one for Moses, and one for Elijah." (He did not know what he was saying, for they were all so frightened.)

Even as he was speaking, a bright cloud appeared overhead and covered them. They grew more frightened as the cloud enveloped them. Suddenly a voice from the cloud said, "This is my beloved Son, in whom I delight. Listen to him!"

When the disciples heard this, they fell on their faces in terror. As soon as the voice had died away, they looked up quickly and glanced around but saw no one with them other than Jesus. Then Jesus touched them and said, "Get up, and don't be afraid."

As they made their way down the mountain, Jesus told them not to tell anyone what they had seen until the Son of Man had risen from the dead. So they kept quiet, telling no one at the time what they had seen and what Jesus had said. Among themselves they discussed what "rising from the dead" might mean.

They also asked Jesus, "Why do the teachers of the law say that Elijah must come first?"

"Elijah is certainly coming first," he answered, "and he will put all things in order. But I'm telling you that Elijah already has come, yet they failed to recognize him and instead did to him anything they wanted—

just as it was predicted. They will subject the Son of Man to the same sort of suffering. Do you remember what is predicted about the Son of Man? It is written that he will suffer many things and be despised."

Finally the disciples understood that he had spoken to them about John the Baptist.

The next day, after they had come down from the mountain, Jesus approached his disciples and saw a large crowd surrounding them as they argued with some teachers of the law. The people were in awe at the sight of him and ran up to welcome him. He asked the teachers of the law, "What are you arguing about?"

In response, a man from the crowd came up to him and dropped to his knees. "Teacher," he said, "I beg you, please look at my son! Have mercy on him—he's my only child! I brought him to you, Lord, because he's an epileptic and suffers terribly from a demon that takes away his speech. Whenever it attacks him, he suddenly screams and falls down in convulsions. He foams at the mouth and grinds his teeth, and it leaves him only after bruising him up. He's wasting away! I brought him to your disciples and begged them to cast it out, but they couldn't cure him."

Then Jesus said, "You obstinate people who refuse to believe—how long will I be with you? How long will I put up with you? Bring your son here to me."

Jesus Healing the Demonized Boy

So they brought the boy to him, but even before he reached him—as soon as the demon saw Jesus—it sent the boy into convulsions, and he fell on the ground, writhing and foaming at the mouth.

Then Jesus asked his father, "How long has this been happening to him?"

"From childhood," he replied. "Many times it has thrown him into the fire and into water to destroy him. But if you can do anything, have pity on us and help us."

Jesus answered, "'If you can'? Everything is possible for the one who believes."

"Lord, I do believe!" the father cried out. "Help me overcome my doubts!"

When Jesus saw that a crowd was running to the scene, he rebuked the demon and said to it, "You deaf and mute demon, I command you to come out of him. And never enter him again!"

After shrieking and throwing the boy into a terrible convulsion, the demon came out. The boy looked so much like a corpse that many people said he was dead. But Jesus took him by the hand and began to lift him, and he got up. Then Jesus gave the boy back to his father. The boy was restored to health from that moment, and they all were astonished at the greatness of God.

After Jesus went into a house, his disciples approached him privately and asked, "Why were we unable to cast it out?"

"Because you have so little genuine faith," Jesus said. "I tell you the truth, if you have faith even the size of a mustard seed, you can say to this mountain, 'Move from here to over there,' and it will move. Nothing will be impossible for you. But this kind will come out only through prayer and fasting."

While everyone was amazed at what Jesus was doing, he said to his disciples, "Listen carefully: the Son of Man will be betrayed into the hands of men!"

They left Caesarea Philippi and traveled through Galilee, but he didn't want anyone to know about it. During their time in Galilee, he continued to teach his disciples, saying, "The Son of Man will be betrayed into human hands, and they will kill him, and after he is killed he will be raised up on the third day."

They were filled with grief, even though they didn't understand what he meant. They were kept from understanding and were afraid to ask him about it.

When they came to Capernaum, the collectors of the half-shekel tax confronted Peter. "Doesn't your teacher intend to pay the half-shekel?" they demanded.

"Yes," Peter replied. "He does."

When he entered the house, Jesus brought up the matter first. "What do you think, Simon?" he asked.

"Do earthly kings collect customs and tribute from their own children or from strangers?"

Peter answered, "From strangers."

"Then the children go free," Jesus replied. "But in order to keep from causing offense, go to the sea and throw in a fishing line. Take the first fish you catch and open its mouth. There you'll find a silver coin."

At that time the disciples came to Jesus in the house and asked him, "Who is the greatest in the kingdom of heaven?" Jesus knew what they were thinking and asked them, "What were you arguing about on our trip?"

They remained silent, because they had been arguing with each other about who would be the greatest.

He sat down and called the twelve together and said, "Whoever wants to be first must be last of all and a servant of all."

Then Jesus called a young child to his side and placed him before them. "I tell you the truth," he said, "unless you change your attitudes and become like little children, you will not be able to enter the kingdom of heaven. The people who humble themselves as this little child are the greatest in the kingdom of heaven. Whoever is least among you will be great.

He took the child in his arms and said to them, "Whoever receives one such little child in my name receives me, and whoever receives me does not receive me, but the one who sent me."

John said to him, "Master, we saw a man casting out demons in your name, and we made him stop because he doesn't follow with us."

"Don't forbid him," Jesus said, "because no one can do a great work in my name and then promptly speak evil of me. Whoever is not against us is for us. I tell you the truth, no one who in my name gives you a cup of water because you belong to Christ will ever lose his reward.

"But if anyone causes one of these little ones who believe in me to sin, it would be better for him to have a big millstone hung around his neck and be sunk in the depths of the sea! What disaster awaits the world for causing someone to sin! It's inevitable that such offense will occur, but what disaster awaits the one who causes it!

"If your hand or foot causes you to sin, cut it off and throw it away! It would be better for you to enter life maimed or lame than to keep your two hands or feet and be thrown into hell, the eternal fire. And if your eye causes you to sin, tear it out and throw it away! It would be better to enter the kingdom of God with one eye than with both eyes to be thrown into hellfire, where their worm never dies and the flames never go out.

"Everyone will be salted with fire. Salt is good, but if the salt has lost its saltiness, how can it regain its flavor? Have salt in yourselves and live in peace with each other.

"Make sure you don't despise one of these little ones, because I'm telling you that their angels in heaven constantly gaze on the face of my heavenly Father. For the Son of Man came to save what was lost.

"What do you think? If a man has a hundred sheep and one gets lost, don't you think he'll leave the ninety-nine and go out on the mountains to look for it? And if he finds it, I tell you the truth, he'll be happier over this one than over the ninety-nine who never wandered away. In the same way, it is not your heavenly Father's will that even one of these little ones should lose his life.

"Now if your brother sins against you, go and tell him privately what he did to you. If he'll listen to you, you have won him back. But if he refuses to listen, take one or two others with you because it takes two or three witnesses to verify any accusation. If he refuses to listen to them, tell it to the congregation. And if he refuses to listen even to them, treat him as you would a pagan or a tax collector.

"I tell you the truth, everything you bind on earth will have been bound in heaven, and everything you release on earth will have been released in heaven.

"I tell you again: if two of you agree on earth about any request at all, my heavenly Father will do it for you. Wherever two or three are gathered in my name, I will be there in the midst of them."

Then Peter approached and said, "Lord, how often do I have to forgive a brother who sins against me? Up to seven times?"

Jesus replied, "Listen to me: not up to seven times, but up to seventy times seven!

"The kingdom of heaven is like a king who decided to make his debtors settle their accounts. In the middle of this settlement, a man was brought to the king who owed a debt worth a great many years in wages. Since he was unable to pay, the king ordered that he be sold as a slave, along with his wife, children, and all his possessions, and that the proceeds be used to cover the debt.

"The man then fell down and pleaded with the king. 'Sir, be patient with me and I'll repay you everything I owe,' he said. The king was moved with compassion, released the man, and forgave him the debt.

"Yet that man went out and found a fellow citizen who owed him a hundred days' wages. He grabbed him by the throat and demanded, 'Pay me back what you owe!' The second man fell at his feet and begged, 'Be patient with me and I'll repay you everything I owe.' But the first man refused and threw him into prison until he could repay the whole debt.

"When the second man's friends saw what had happened, they were furious. They went to tell their king what had taken place. The king sent for the first man and said, 'You wicked peasant! I forgave you your entire debt when you pleaded with me. Shouldn't you have shown mercy to your fellow citizen, just as I showed mercy to you?' In a rage the king turned the man over to the jailers until he could pay back every cent he owed.

"My heavenly Father will do the same with you unless each of you forgives your brother from your heart."

When Jesus finished speaking, he got up, left Galilee, and went to the region of Judea on the other side of the Jordan. Large crowds surrounded him again and began to follow him. And, as was his custom, he taught them and healed them.

As the time approached for Jesus to be taken up to heaven, he made a firm decision to go to Jerusalem. He sent messengers ahead of him, and they entered a

Samaritan village to make preparations for him. But the people there would not welcome him because it was clear he was heading for Jerusalem.

When his disciples James and John saw what was happening, they said, "Lord, do you want us to call down fire from heaven and burn them up?"

He turned and rebuked them, saying, "You don't realize what spirit you are reflecting. For the Son of Man came not to destroy men's lives but to save them." So they went to another village.

As they were on their way, a teacher of the law approached and said, "Teacher, I'll follow you wherever you go."

"The foxes have holes and the birds have nests," Jesus replied, "but the Son of Man has no place to rest his head."

Jesus said to one of his disciples, "Follow me."

"Lord," the man said, "allow me first to go bury my father."

"Let the dead bury their own dead," Jesus answered. "But you go out and announce the kingdom of God!"

Another man said, "I'll follow you, Lord, but first let me say good-bye to my family."

Jesus said to him, "No one who has started to plow and looks back is fit for the kingdom of God."

Afterward the Lord commissioned seventy others and sent them out in pairs to go ahead of him into every city and place he intended to visit.

"The harvest indeed is plentiful," he said, "but the workers are few. Therefore earnestly ask the Lord of the harvest to send out workers into his harvest.

"Go on your way. Look, I am sending you out like lambs among a pack of wolves. Don't carry a purse or a bag or sandals, and don't greet anyone on the way. Whenever you enter a home, first say, 'Peace to this home.' If a person of peace really lives there, your peace will rest on him. If not, your peace will return to you. Remain in that home, eating and drinking whatever they provide for you, because the worker deserves his wages. Don't move from home to home.

"Whenever you enter a city and they welcome you, eat whatever they place in front of you. Heal the sick there and say to them, 'The kingdom of God has come near.' But if you should enter a city that doesn't welcome you, go out into its streets and say, 'As a testimony against you we are wiping off the dust of your city that clings to us. But understand that the kingdom of God has come near you.' I'm telling you that on the judgment day the land of Sodom will be better off than that city."

Then he began denouncing the cities where he had done most of his miracles, because they did not turn from their sin. "Disaster awaits you, Chorazin! Disaster awaits you, Bethsaida! If the great miracles performed in you had been done in Tyre and Sidon, they would have turned from their sin long ago and be sitting in sackcloth and ashes. I'm telling you, it will be better for Tyre and Sidon on the judgment day than for you!

"And you, Capernaum—have you been lifted up to heaven? You'll be thrown down into hell! For if the great miracles performed in you had been done in Sodom, it would still exist today. So I tell you the same thing: it will be better for the land of Sodom on the judgment day than for you!

"Whoever listens to you listens to me, and whoever rejects you rejects me. And whoever rejects me rejects the one who sent me."

When the seventy returned, they joyfully reported, "Lord, even the demons submit to our authority when we act in your name!"

But Jesus said, "I saw Satan falling like lightning from heaven. I give you the authority to walk on snakes and scorpions and over all the enemy's power. Nothing will hurt you in any way. Nevertheless, don't rejoice in the fact that the demons submit to your authority, but rejoice that your names are recorded in heaven."

At that moment Jesus rejoiced in the Holy Spirit, saying, "I praise you, O Father, Lord of heaven and earth, that you've hidden these things from educated and smart people and revealed them to infants. Yes, Father, this gave you great pleasure.

"Everything has been committed to me by my Father.

"Nobody knows who the Son is except the Father, and nobody knows who the Father is except the Son and those to whom the Son chooses to reveal him.

"Come to me, everyone who is weary and carrying a heavy load, and I'll give you rest. Put my yoke upon you and learn about me. I am gentle and humble in heart, and you'll find rest for your souls. For my yoke is easy and my load is light."

Then in private he turned to his disciples and said, "The eyes that see what you see are greatly blessed! I'm telling you that many prophets and kings wanted to see the things you see yet didn't see them—and to hear the things you hear but didn't hear them."

Then a certain expert in the law stood up to test Jesus. "Teacher," he said, "what must I do to inherit eternal life?"

"What was written in the law?" Jesus replied. "How do you interpret it?"

The man answered, "'You shall love the Lord your God with all your heart and with all your soul and with all your strength and with all your mind.' And, 'Love your neighbor as yourself.'"

"Your answer is correct," Jesus said. "Act accordingly, and you will live."

Then the man, wanting to justify himself, said to Jesus, "And who exactly is my neighbor?"

Accepting the challenge, Jesus said, "A man once took a trip from Jerusalem down to Jericho. Along the way robbers attacked him, stripped off his clothes, and beat him, then went away, leaving him half dead.

"Soon a certain priest happened to take the same road. When he saw the man, he crossed to the other side and kept going. Not long afterward a Levite came to the same place, saw the man, and also passed by on the other side.

"But then a traveling Samaritan came by, and when he saw the man, he was filled with pity. He examined him and dressed his wounds, applying wine and oil to them. Then he put the man on his own donkey and brought him to an inn, where he took care of him. When he left the following day, he took out two days' wages and gave the money to the innkeeper. 'Take care of him,' he instructed, 'and I'll repay you for whatever else you may spend.'

"Now then, which of these three men do you think was a neighbor to the man who was robbed?"

The expert in the law replied, "The man who showed kindness."

"Go," Jesus said, "and act in the same way."

As they continued their journey, Jesus entered a certain village where a woman named Martha welcomed him into her home. She had a sister named Mary, who sat at the feet of Jesus and kept listening to what he said.

Martha was distracted with all the details of serving her guests. Finally she approached Jesus and said, "Lord, does it not bother you that my sister has left me to do all the work alone? Tell her to help me!"

"Martha, Martha," Jesus answered. "You're anxious and worried about many things, but only one thing is necessary. Mary has chosen the good part, and it won't be taken away from her."

As Jesus finished praying one day in a certain place, one of his disciples said to him, "Lord, teach us to pray, just as John taught his disciples."

So Jesus said to them, "When you pray, say,
'Father, may your name be held in awe.
May your kingdom come.
[May your will be done
  on earth as it is in heaven.]
Give us the bread we need each day.

And forgive us our sins,
for we forgive everyone who sins against us.
And do not allow us to be led into temptation.
But deliver us from evil.' "

He continued, "Suppose you must go to a friend at midnight and say, 'my friend, may I borrow three loaves of bread? An acquaintance on a journey has just arrived and I have nothing for him to eat.' What kind of friend would answer, 'Don't bother me? I've already locked up the house for the night and my children are tucked into bed. I can't get up to give you anything'? I'm telling you that even if he won't get up and offer help for the sake of their friendship, yet because of his friend's bold persistence, he'll arise and give him whatever he needs.

"And I tell you, ask, and you'll receive. Seek, and you'll find. Knock, and the door will be opened for you. For everyone who asks, receives; and whoever seeks, finds; and the one who knocks will discover an open door.

"If your son should ask you for bread, which of you fathers would give him a stone? Or if he asks for fish, which of you would hand him a snake? Or if he asks for an egg, who would give him a scorpion? If you know how to give good gifts to your children—even though you're evil—how much more will the heavenly Father give the Holy Spirit to those who ask him!"

Then Jesus cast a demon out of a man made dumb, enabling him to speak after the demon left. This filled the multitude with awe. But some charged, "He casts out demons by Beelzebul, the prince of the demons." Others challenged him to show a sign from heaven.

Jesus knew what they were thinking and said to them, "Every nation that fights against itself causes its own ruin. In the same way, a house that fights against itself cannot survive. So if Satan is divided against himself, how will his kingdom survive?

"You say that I cast out demons by the power of Beelzebul. But if I by Beelzebul cast out demons, through whom do your sons do the same thing? They shall be your judges in this. But if through the finger of God I cast out demons, then the kingdom of God has come upon you!

"When a strong man fully armed protects his property, his possessions are safe. But when one stronger than he comes and overpowers him, both the weapons that gave him confidence and all his property will be taken away. Whoever is not with me is against me, and he that does not gather with me scatters.

"When a demon leaves a person, it passes through desolate areas in search of a place of rest. Not finding one, it says, 'I'll return to the house from which I came.' When it does, it finds it swept clean and put in order. Then it goes out and recruits seven other demons who are even more wicked, and they settle in and live there. The end result is that the person's last condition is worse than the first."

As he was speaking, a woman from the crowd shouted, "How blessed is the womb that bore you and the breasts at which you nursed!"

"Not true!" Jesus replied. "Rather, blessed are those who hear the word of God and obey it."

As the crowds were increasing, Jesus began to say to them: "This generation is a wicked one! It seeks for signs, but no miraculous signs will be given it except the sign of the prophet Jonah. Just as Jonah himself became a sign to the residents of Nineveh, so shall the Son of Man be to this generation.

"The queen of the South will stand up at the judgment and condemn this generation, for she came from the ends of the earth to hear the wisdom of Solomon. Yet someone greater than Solomon is here. The men of Nineveh will stand up with this generation at the judgment and condemn it, because they repented at the preaching of Jonah. Yet someone greater than Jonah is here.

"Nobody lights a lamp and puts it in a hiding place or under a basket but on a lamp stand where everyone entering the house can see its light. The eye is the lamp of the body. So if your eye is healthy your whole body will be filled with light, but if your eye is diseased your whole body will be filled with darkness. Therefore make sure that the light in you is not actually darkness! On the other hand, if your body is filled with light, with no dark corners anywhere, it will be completely illuminated—like the glowing lamp that gives you light."

As Jesus was speaking, a Pharisee invited him to dinner. He accepted and reclined at the table. When the Pharisee saw this, he was shocked that Jesus did not ceremonially wash before dinner.

Then the Lord said to him, "You Pharisees carefully clean the outside of the cup and the platter, but inside you're full of robbery and wickedness. You foolish people! Didn't the one who made the outside make the inside, too? Give [to the poor] from the abundance of your heart, then everything will be clean for you.

"But destruction awaits you, Pharisees! You give God a tenth of your mint and rue and other herbs, yet you disregard justice and love for God! You should have done the former without leaving the latter undone.

"Destruction awaits you, Pharisees! You love the most prominent seats in the synagogues, and to be greeted in the marketplaces. Destruction awaits you!

You're like unmarked graves, which people walk over without realizing it."

Then one of the experts on the law answered, "Teacher, you also insult us when you say these things."

He replied, "Destruction awaits you experts on the law as well! You weigh people down with impossible burdens while you yourselves refuse to lift a finger to help. Destruction awaits you because you build the tombs of the prophets whom your ancestors murdered! In this way you affirm and approve the actions of your ancestors—they murdered them, and you build their tombs.

"That is why God in his wisdom said, 'I will send them prophets and apostles, some of whom they will kill and persecute.' Therefore the guilt for shedding the blood of all the prophets since the creation of the world will be laid to the account of this generation. I tell you the truth, all this guilt—from the blood of Abel to the blood of Zechariah, who died between the altar and the sanctuary—will be laid to the account of this generation.

"Destruction awaits you experts on the law! You have taken away the key to knowledge. You yourselves did not enter and you have hindered those who tried to enter."

After he said these things, the teachers of the law and Pharisees began to oppose him fiercely. They questioned him on many points, lying in wait to trap him in something he said.

As the crowds grew so large that people were trampling each other, Jesus began saying to his disciples, "Watch out for the yeast of the Pharisees, which is hypocrisy. There is nothing covered up that won't be uncovered, and nothing hidden that won't be revealed. Everything you have said in the dark will be broadcast in broad daylight, and what you have whispered in private rooms will be shouted on the housetops.

"My friends, I'm telling you not to be afraid of those who kill the body but can do nothing worse. I will tell you whom to fear instead: fear the one who can both kill you and throw you into hell. Yes, be afraid of him!

"Aren't five sparrows sold for two pennies? Yet God doesn't overlook a single one of them. Even the hairs on your head are all numbered! So don't be afraid; you're far more precious than many sparrows.

"I must tell you that everyone who acknowledges me before others will also be acknowledged by the Son of Man before the angels of God. But the one who denies me before others will be denied before the angels of God.

"While there is forgiveness for everyone who speaks a word against the Son of Man, he that blasphemes the Holy Spirit shall never be forgiven.

"When they bring you before synagogues, rulers, and authorities, don't worry beforehand how or what you should say in your defense. In that hour the Holy Spirit will instruct you what you should say."

Someone in the crowd said to Jesus, "Teacher, command my brother to divide the inheritance with me." Jesus replied, "Man, who made me a judge or an arbiter over you?"

Then he said to them all, "Watch out! Be on your guard against greed of all kinds. A person's life is not the sum total of his possessions."

Then he told them a parable: "A rich man's land yielded an abundant crop. So he asked himself, 'What should I do? I've run out of room to store my crops.' So he said, 'I'll do this: I'll tear down my barns and build bigger ones. That's where I'll store all my produce and my possessions. And I'll tell myself, "You've stored enough away to last you many years. So take it easy—eat, drink, and be merry!"'

"But God said to him, 'You fool! This very night your life is to be taken from you. And then who will enjoy the things you have hoarded?'

"That is the way it will be for everyone who hoards treasure for himself but isn't rich toward God.

"Don't be afraid, little flock," Jesus told his disciples, "because the Father is delighted to give you the kingdom. Sell your possessions and give to the poor. Provide money bags for yourselves that don't wear out—a heavenly treasure that is never used up, where no thief comes close and no moth destroys. For your heart will be found wherever you keep your treasure.

"Be dressed and ready and keep your lamps burning. Be like those who are waiting for their master to return from a wedding feast. As soon as he arrives and knocks, they can open the door immediately.

"Those servants who are watching when the Lord returns will be especially blessed. I tell you the truth, he will get dressed to wait on them himself as they recline to eat. So whether he comes before or after midnight, those servants who are ready will be blessed!

"But remember this: if the homeowner had known what time of night the thief would come, he would have watched and prevented his house from being burglarized. In the same way you should be ready, because the Son of Man will come just when you think he won't."

Then Peter asked him, "Lord, are you telling this parable to everyone, or just to us?"

The Lord replied, "Who is the trustworthy and wise manager whose master will put him in charge of the whole household, to make sure everyone is fed properly? That servant who is found to be doing so when his master comes will be blessed. I tell you the truth, he'll put him in charge of everything he owns.

"But suppose that wicked servant says to himself, 'My master's return is delayed,' and he begins to beat his fellow servants, both men and women, and to eat and drink and get drunk. His master will come on the day he least expects it, at an hour he doesn't imagine, and will cut him in pieces and assign him a place with the hypocrites and unbelievers.

"That servant who knew what his master wanted him to do but did not prepare accordingly will be whipped with many lashes. But the one who didn't know, and yet did things deserving such punishment, will be whipped with only a few. Whoever has been given much will be required to produce much, and whoever was entrusted with much will be asked to contribute much.

"I came to bring fire on the earth, and how I wish it were already kindled! I also have a baptism to undergo, and how distressed I am until it is accomplished!

"Do you think I came to bring peace to the earth? No, I came to cause division. I did not come to bring peace but rather a sword. From now on in a single home five people will be divided against each other—three against two, and two against three. I came to set a son against his father and a father against his son, a daughter against her mother and a mother against her daughter, a daughter-in-law against her mother-in-law and a mother-in-law against her daughter-in-law. A person's enemies will come from his own household."

Jesus also said to the crowds, "When you see clouds rising from the west, you immediately say, 'A shower is coming,' and it does. And when a south wind is blowing, you say, 'It will be hot,' and it is. You hypocrites! You know how to interpret the appearance of earth and sky, so why don't you know how to interpret this present time?

"Why don't you judge for yourselves what is right? When you're heading to court with someone who has filed suit against you, try hard to reach a settlement before you arrive. Otherwise he may drag you to the judge, and the judge will hand you over to the police, and the police will throw you into jail. The truth is, you won't get out of there until you've paid the last cent of what you owe!"

Some people there told him about the Galileans whose blood Pilate had mixed with their sacrifices. Jesus answered, "Do you think these Galileans were worse sinners than all the other Galileans simply because they suffered so terribly? That's not true, I tell you! But unless you turn from your sins, you will all suffer a similar fate!

"Or those eighteen people who were killed when the tower of Siloam fell on them—do you think they were worse sinners than anyone else living in Jerusalem? I tell you, it's not true! But unless you turn from your sins, you will all suffer a similar fate!"

Then he told them a parable: "A man had a fig tree planted in his vineyard. He came looking for fruit on it but found none. Then he said to the caretaker of the vineyard, 'Look, for three years I've been coming to get fruit from this fig tree but have found none. Cut it down! Why should it use up good ground?'

"But the caretaker replied, 'Sir, let the tree grow for another year as well, so I can dig around it and fertilize it. If it bears fruit, fine. But if it doesn't, you can cut it down.'"

One Sabbath day when Jesus was teaching in a synagogue, a woman was there who had been crippled by a demon for eighteen years. She was doubled over and couldn't straighten up. When Jesus saw her, he called out to her and said, "Woman, you are healed from your affliction."

As soon as he laid his hands on her, she could stand up straight, and she began to praise God.

The ruler of the synagogue was angry with Jesus for healing on the Sabbath and said to the people, "There are six days set aside for working. Come on one of those days to be healed and not on the Sabbath."

The Lord replied, "You hypocrite! Even on the Sabbath each one of you here unties his ox or his donkey from the stall and leads it to water. So shouldn't this woman—a descendant of Abraham who has been bound by Satan for eighteen years— be freed on the Sabbath day from what bound her?"

His reply embarrassed his opponents, while the crowd kept rejoicing at all the wonderful things he did.

"What is the kingdom of God like?" Jesus said. "To what can I compare it? It's like a mustard seed that a man planted in his garden. It grew and became a tree, and birds came down from the sky to roost in its branches."

He said again, "To what can I compare the kingdom of God? It's like yeast that a woman took and hid in three measures of flour until the whole mixture was leavened."

So Jesus traveled on through many cities and villages, teaching and making his way to Jerusalem.

Then someone said to him, "Lord, will only a few be saved?"

"Try hard to enter through the narrow gate," he replied. "I'm telling you that many will try to enter but won't be able to. Once the master of the house has arisen and shut the door, you will stand outside knocking and say, 'Lord, Lord, open the door for us!' But he'll answer, 'I don't know who you are. Where are you from?' You'll reply, 'We ate and drank with you, and you taught in our streets.' And he will say, 'I'm telling you again, I don't know who you are or where you're from. Get away from me, all you who do evil!'

"There will be weeping there and gnashing of teeth when you see Abraham and Isaac and Jacob and all the prophets in the kingdom of God, but you yourselves thrown out. People will come from the East and the West, and from the North and the South, to feast in the kingdom of God. Understand this: some who are last will be first, and some who are first will be last."

That day some Pharisees came to him and said, "Leave at once, and get away from here! Herod intends to kill you."

He said to them, "Go and tell that fox, 'Look, today and tomorrow I'm casting out demons and healing people, and the third day I will reach my destination.' Even so, I must move ahead today and tomorrow and the day after. How unthinkable that a prophet should die anywhere but in Jerusalem!

"O Jerusalem, Jerusalem! You who have killed the prophets and stoned those who were sent to you! How often I would have gathered your children, as a hen gathers her brood under her wings—and you refused! Look! Your house will be left desolate. I tell the truth, you will not see me anymore until you say, 'Blessed is the one who comes in the name of the Lord!'"

Jesus went to dinner one Sabbath at the home of a leading Pharisee, and they were watching him closely. A man with dropsy was there, and Jesus asked the experts on the law and Pharisees, "Is it legal to heal on the Sabbath?"

But they kept silent.

Jesus took hold of the man, healed him, and sent him away. Then he said to them, "Which of you on the Sabbath day would not immediately pull out one of your oxen or donkeys that fell into a pit?"

None of them could make a reply.

When he noted how the guests were choosing the best places at the table, he told them a parable: "When you're invited to a wedding feast, don't take the place of honor. Otherwise if someone more prominent than you is also a guest, the one who invited you both may say to you, 'Give this man your place.' Then in humiliation you'll have to sit in the least important place. Instead, when you're invited, take the least important place. When the one who invited you arrives, he may say to you, 'My friend, move up to a better place,' and you'll be honored in front of all. For everyone who elevates himself will be humbled, and the one who humbles himself will be elevated."

Then he said to the one who invited him, "When you hold a dinner or a banquet, don't call your friends or your brothers or your relatives or rich neighbors. For they will return the invitation, and so repay you. But when you hold a feast, invite the poor, the crippled, the lame, and the blind. Then you'll be blessed because they can't repay you. You'll be repaid at the resurrection of the godly."

When one of the dinner guests heard this, he said to Jesus, "Blessed is the one who will eat bread in the kingdom of God!"

Jesus replied, "A man was preparing a large banquet and sent out many invitations. When the date arrived, he sent his servant to tell the guests, 'It's time to come. Everything is ready.' But all of them together began making excuses. The first said to him, 'I just bought a field, and I must go see it. Please, send my regrets.'

Another said, 'I just bought five yoke of oxen, and I'm leaving to try them out. Please excuse me.' Yet another said, 'I just got married, so I can't come.'

"When the servant reported back to his master, the master angrily told his servant, 'Quickly! Go out into the streets and alleys of the city and bring in the poor, the crippled, the lame, and the blind.' The servant replied, 'Sir, we've already done what you commanded, but there's still room.' The master said to the servant, 'Then go out to the highways and the outskirts of town and compel them to come in, so my house will be full! But believe me, not one of the guests who were first invited will taste a single morsel of my banquet!'"

Large crowds were walking along with Jesus, and he turned and said to them, "Anyone who comes to me but doesn't hate his father and mother, and wife and children, and brothers and sisters, and even his own life, cannot be my disciple. And whoever refuses to bear his cross and follow me cannot be my disciple.

"Suppose you want to build a tower. Which of you would not first sit down and calculate the cost to make sure you have enough to finish the project? Otherwise if you're forced to stop after you have laid its foundation, everyone who sees it will laugh at you and say, 'This man began to build but was unable to finish.'

"Or what king who intended to start a war with some other king would not first sit down and consider whether his army of ten thousand could fight an army of twenty thousand? If he can't, while his opponent is still far away, he'll send a delegation to ask for terms of peace.

"In the same way, whoever of you does not leave everything he has cannot be my disciple. Salt is good, but if the salt loses its saltiness, how can it be seasoned again? It's fit neither for the land nor for the manure pile. People throw it out. Whoever has ears to hear, let him hear!"

All the tax collectors and sinful outcasts continued to come and hear him, while the Pharisees and teachers of the law kept muttering, "This man welcomes sinners and eats with them!"

So he told them this parable: "Suppose one of you has a hundred sheep and one of them gets lost. Will he not leave the ninety-nine in the desert and search for the lost one until he finds it? And when he finds it, he lays it joyfully on his shoulders. When he gets home, he calls together his friends and neighbors and tells them, 'Celebrate with me because I found the sheep that was lost!' I'm telling you there will be more joy like that in heaven for one sinner who repents than for ninety-nine righteous people who don't need to repent.

"Or suppose a woman has ten silver coins and loses one. Won't she light a lamp and sweep the house and search carefully until it's found? When she finds it, she calls together friends and neighbors and says, 'Celebrate with me because I found the coin I lost!' In the same way, I'm telling you, there is great joy in the presence of God's angels for one sinner who repents."

Then Jesus said, "A certain man had two sons. The younger of them said to his father, 'Father, give me the portion of the estate that's coming to me.' So the father parceled out the inheritance.

"A few days later the younger son gathered all he owned and left for a distant country. There he squandered his wealth in wild living. When all his money was gone, a severe famine swept the country, and he began to be in severe need. He took a job with a citizen of that country who sent him into the fields to feed pigs. The young man longed to satisfy his hunger with the food the pigs were eating, but no one offered him anything.

"When he came to his senses, he said, 'My father's hired servants have bread to spare while I'm starving! I'll get up and go to my father and say to him, "Father, I have sinned against both God and you, and I'm no longer worthy to be called your son. But please make me like one of your hired servants."' So he got up and went to his father.

"While he was still a long way off, his father saw him and was filled with compassion for him. He ran to him, threw his arms around him, and kissed him repeatedly. Then the son said to him, 'Father, I have sinned against both God and you, and I'm no longer worthy to be called your son.'

"But the father said to his servants, 'Bring out the best robe and put it on him, and put a ring on his hand and sandals on his feet. And get the fattened calf and kill it, and let us eat and celebrate. For this son of mine was dead, but he's alive again. He was lost, but he has been found!' So they began to celebrate."

Now the elder son was out in the field, and as he approached the house, he heard music and dancing. So he called one of the servants and asked what was going on. The man replied, 'Your brother has come home! Your father has killed the fattened calf because he has returned safe and sound.'

"But the elder brother was angry and wouldn't join the festivities. When his father came out to plead with him, the son said, 'Look, for many years I've served you, and I never disobeyed you. But you never gave me even a goat so I could celebrate with my friends! Yet when this son of yours comes home—somebody who wasted your money on prostitutes—for him you kill the fattened calf.'

The Prodigal Son in the Arms of His Father

"The father answered, 'Son, you are always with me and everything I have is yours. But it was right that we should celebrate and be glad. Your brother was dead, but he's alive again! And he was lost, but he's been found!'"

Jesus also said to his disciples, "A rich man received a report that his manager was wasting his funds. Therefore the rich man summoned him and asked, 'What is this I hear about you? Give me a full account of your management, for you are relieved of your duties.'

"Then the manager said to himself, 'What will I do now since my master is taking away my position? I cannot dig, and I'd be too ashamed to beg. I know what I'll do so that when I lose my position, people will take me into their homes.'

"He called in everyone who was indebted to his master. He said to the first one, 'How much do you owe my master?' The man replied, 'Eight hundred gallons of oil.' The manager said, 'Sit down quickly and make your bill four hundred.' Then he said to another man, 'And how much do you owe?' The man replied, 'A thousand bushels of wheat.' He told him, 'Take your bill and make it eight hundred.'

"The master commended his dishonest manager because he had acted shrewdly. For the people of this world are wiser in dealing with their own kind than are the people of light. So I tell you, use worldly wealth to make friends for yourselves, so that when it runs out, they will welcome you into eternal homes.

"Whoever is faithful in the smallest of things is also faithful in big things, but whoever is untrustworthy in the smallest things is also untrustworthy in big things. So if you have proven untrustworthy with worldly wealth, who will trust you with heavenly riches? And if you haven't been faithful with someone else's possessions, who would give you something of your own?

"No servant can serve two masters. Either he will hate one and love the other, or he will cling to one and despise the other. You cannot serve both God and riches."

The Pharisees, who loved money, were listening to all of this, and they sneered at Jesus. He answered them, "You are the ones who make yourselves look holy in the eyes of others. But God knows your hearts! What people regard highly is abominable in God's eyes.

"The law and the prophets were preached until John; since then the kingdom of God is being preached, and everyone is forcing his way into it. But it would be easier for heaven and earth to vanish than for one speck of the law to disappear."

And he said, "Everyone who divorces his wife and marries another commits adultery. And the man who marries a divorced woman commits adultery.

"There was a certain rich man," he continued, "who dressed in expensive and beautiful clothes and lived in luxury. A poor man named Lazarus was laid at his gate, full of sores and longing to eat the crumbs that fell from the rich man's table. Even the dogs came and licked his sores.

"One day the poor man died, and the angels carried him away to Abraham's side. The rich man also died and was buried. In torment in the place of the dead, he looked up and saw Abraham a long way off with Lazarus at his side. He cried out, 'Father Abraham, take pity on me! Send Lazarus to dip his fingertip in water and cool my tongue. I am in agony in this flame!'

"But Abraham replied, 'Son, remember that in your lifetime you enjoyed many good things, while Lazarus suffered. Now he is comforted, while you're in agony. And besides, a huge chasm lies between us and you that makes it impossible for anyone to cross from here to you or from there to us.'

"'Then father, I beg you!' said the rich man. 'Send Lazarus to my father's house, where my five brothers live. Have him tell them about this place of torment, so they don't come here, too!'

"'They have Moses and the prophets,' Abraham replied. 'Let them listen to them.'

"He responded, 'That's not enough, father Abraham. But if someone from the dead goes to them, they will repent.'

"And Abraham answered, 'If they won't listen to Moses and the prophets, neither will they be persuaded by someone who has risen from the dead.'"

Then Jesus said to the disciples, "Things that cause people to sin will inevitably come. But disaster awaits the person through whom they come! It would be better for him if a huge millstone were hung around his neck, and he were thrown into the sea, than that he should cause one of these little ones to stumble. Watch yourselves!

"If your brother sins against you, rebuke him, and if he repents, forgive him. Even if he sins against you seven times in one day and each time comes to you and says, 'I repent,' you are to forgive him."

The disciples replied to the Lord, "Increase our faith!"

The Lord said to them, "If you had faith the size of a mustard seed, you could say to this mulberry tree, 'Tear yourself out of the ground and plant yourself in the sea,' and it would obey you.

"Would any of you say to a servant who was returning from plowing or tending sheep, 'Come on in and sit right down for dinner'? Rather, will you not say to him, 'Prepare my food and get dressed to serve me while I eat and drink. Afterward you can eat and drink'? Will that servant be thanked because he did what he was told? Certainly not. In the same way, when you have done everything you were told to do, say this: 'We are unworthy servants; we have only done our duty.'"

On his way to Jerusalem, Jesus traveled along the border of Samaria and Galilee. When he entered a village, ten lepers met him, standing at a distance. They cried out, "Jesus, master, have pity on us!"

When he saw them he said, "Go on your way and show yourselves to the priests."

As they were leaving, they were healed. Seeing that he was well, one of them turned back and loudly praised God. He fell at Jesus' feet and thanked him. The man was a Samaritan.

"Were not ten men healed?" Jesus asked. "Where are the other nine? Could none of them return to give God glory except this foreigner?" So he said to the man, "Get up and go on your way. Your faith has healed you."

One day the Pharisees asked Jesus when the kingdom of God would arrive. He answered, "The kingdom of God doesn't come with visible signs. No one will say, 'Look, it's right here!' or 'Look over there!' because the kingdom of God is within you."

He said to the disciples, "The time is coming when you will long to see one of the days of the Son of Man, yet you will not see it. They will say to you, 'Look, it's right here!' or 'Look over there!' Don't go out and follow them. Just as lightning flashes from one end of the sky to the other, so the Son of Man will be in his day. First, however, he must suffer many things and be rejected by this generation.

"The days of the Son of Man will be just like the days of Noah. They were eating and drinking, getting married and being given in marriage, until the day Noah went into the ark, and the flood came and destroyed them all.

"It will also be just like the days of Lot. They were eating and drinking, buying and selling, planting and building. But the day Lot left Sodom, fire and sulfur rained down from the sky and destroyed them all. It will be like that on the day the Son of Man is revealed. When that day comes, no one on the housetop should come down to collect his possessions in the house. And no one in the field should return to the things he left behind. Remember Lot's wife! Whoever tries to save his life will lose it, but whoever loses his life will save it.

"I'm telling you that on that night two men will be in the same room; one will be taken, and the other left. Two women will be working in the same kitchen; one will be taken and the other left. Likewise with two men in the yard; one will be taken and the other left."

They then asked him, "Where, Lord?"

He replied, "Where the body lies, there the vultures will gather."

Jesus also told a parable about how they should always pray and not lose heart: "In a certain city there was a judge who didn't fear God or respect people. A widow kept coming to him and demanding, 'Grant me justice against my adversary!' For a while he refused to do so, but after a long time he said to himself, 'Even though I don't fear God or respect people, yet I will grant justice to this bothersome widow. Her constant petitions are wearing me out!'

"Listen to what the unjust judge said. Do you suppose God will refuse to grant justice to his people who cry out to him day and night? Do you think he'll keep delaying in giving them help? I'm telling you that he will grant them justice, and quickly!

"But when the Son of Man comes, will he find faith on the earth?"

He also told a parable to people who trusted in their own righteousness and looked down on others: "Two men went into the temple to pray. One was a Pharisee, the other a tax collector. The Pharisee stood up and prayed to himself like this: 'God, I thank you that I'm not like other men—greedy, ungodly, adulterous— or even like this tax collector. I fast twice each week and give you a tenth of everything I get.'

"But the tax collector stood at a distance and wouldn't even look up to heaven. Instead he kept pounding his chest and saying, 'God, be merciful to me, for I'm a sinner!'

"I'm telling you, this man went home justified before God, and not the other man. For everyone who elevates himself will be humbled, while the one who humbles himself will be elevated."

Then some Pharisees came to test him. They asked, "Is it legal for a husband to divorce his wife, for any reason at all?"

"What did Moses command you?" Jesus responded. "Haven't you read that the Creator made them male and female and said, 'This is why a man is to leave his father and mother and be united to his wife, and the two will become one'? So you see, they are no longer two, but one. Therefore, what God has united, let no one pull apart."

Jesus Blessing the Little Children

"Then why," they replied, "did Moses command that she be given a document of divorce and sent away?"

He answered, "It was only because your hearts were hard that Moses wrote this law and allowed you to divorce your wives. Yet it wasn't this way from the very beginning! I'm telling you that whoever divorces his wife, except on the grounds of sexual unfaithfulness, and marries someone else, commits adultery."

"If this is the way it is between a man and his wife," his disciples replied, "it would be better not to marry."

"Not everyone can accept this," Jesus told them. "In fact, only those to whom it has been granted can do so. There are eunuchs who were born that way and there are eunuchs who were made that way by people. There are yet others who have made themselves eunuchs for the sake of the kingdom of heaven. Whoever can accept this, let him accept it."

Once more back in the house, his disciples asked him about this. He said to them, "Whoever divorces his wife and marries someone else is committing adultery against her. And if a woman divorces her husband and marries someone else, she is committing adultery."

At that time young children were being brought to Jesus so he could lay his hands on them and pray for them. People were even bringing him infants to touch. When the disciples saw what was happening, they began to scold those who brought them.

Jesus was indignant when he saw this. He called them together and said, "Let the little children come to me and never stop them. Why, the kingdom of heaven is made up of people like them! I tell you the truth, anyone who refuses to accept the kingdom of God in the same way that a little child does will never enter it."

Then he swept the children up in his arms, laid his hands on them, and blessed them.

A man named Lazarus was sick. He was from Bethany, the village of Mary and her sister Martha. (This was the same Mary who anointed the Lord with ointment and wiped his feet with her hair. It was her brother Lazarus who was sick.) The sisters sent word to Jesus, "Lord, the one you love is sick."

When Jesus heard this, he said, "This sickness will not end in death. Instead it will show the glory of God, and through it the Son of Man will be glorified."

Now Jesus loved Martha and her sister and Lazarus. Yet when he heard that he was sick, he stayed two more days where he was. Afterward he said to his disciples, "Let's return to Judea."

"Rabbi," the disciples replied, "not long ago the Jews were trying to stone you. Why are you going there again?"

"Aren't there twelve hours of daylight?" Jesus told them. "Whoever walks in the daytime avoids stumbling since he sees the light of the world. But anyone who walks at night stumbles since the light is not in him."

Then he added, "Our friend Lazarus has fallen asleep. I am going to wake him up."

Then his disciples said, "Lord, if he has fallen asleep, he'll get better." Jesus had spoken of his death, but his disciples thought he was talking about literal sleep.

Then Jesus said to them plainly, "Lazarus is dead. And for your sake I'm glad I wasn't there. Now you will have the opportunity to believe. But let us go to him."

Thomas (also called Didymus) said to his fellow disciples, "Let's go, too, so we may die with him."

When Jesus arrived, he found that Lazarus already had been in the tomb for four days. Since Bethany was near Jerusalem (less than two miles away), many Jews had come to Martha and Mary to comfort them about their brother's death.

As soon as Martha heard that Jesus was coming, she hurried out to meet him while Mary continued sitting in the house. Martha said to Jesus, "Lord, if you had been here my brother would not have died! Yet even now I know that God will give you anything you ask for."

Jesus said to her, "Your brother will rise again."

"I know that he will rise again in the resurrection at the end of time," Martha replied.

Jesus said to her, "I am the resurrection and the life. Whoever believes in me will live even if he should die. And whoever lives and believes in me shall never die. Do you believe this?"

"Yes, Lord!" she answered. "I, too, have believed that you're the Messiah, the Son of God who was to come into the world."

Then she left and called her sister Mary. "The teacher has come," she told her privately, "and is asking for you."

When Mary heard this, she got up and came to him. (Jesus had not yet arrived in the village but remained where Martha met him.) When the Jews who had come to the house to comfort Mary saw her get up quickly and leave, they followed her, thinking she was going to the tomb to weep there.

As soon as Mary reached Jesus, she fell at his feet. "Lord," she said, "if you had been here my brother would not have died."

When Jesus saw both her and the Jews weeping, he sighed deeply and was troubled. "Where have you laid him?" he asked. "Lord, come and see," they answered.

Jesus wept.

"Look how much he loved him!" the Jews said. Yet some of them remarked, "Couldn't the man who gave sight to the blind have kept this man from dying?"

Jesus sighed deeply once more as he came to the tomb. It was a cave, with a stone covering the entrance. "Take away the stone," Jesus said.

"Lord, by this time there is a stench," replied Martha, the dead man's sister. "It's been four days."

"Didn't I tell you," said Jesus, "that if you believe, you would see the glory of God?"

So they removed the stone from the place they had laid the dead man.

Jesus looked up to heaven and said, "Father, I thank you that you heard me. I knew you always hear me, but I said it because of the crowd standing here, so they may believe you really sent me."

Then Jesus shouted, "Lazarus, come out!"

The one who had been dead came out, wrapped tightly from head to toe in strips of linen, and his face wrapped in a cloth. "Take off the grave clothes," Jesus said to the people there, "and let him go."

Many of the Jews who visited Mary and saw what Jesus did believed in him. But others went to the Pharisees and told them what Jesus had done. Then the chief priests and the Pharisees called a meeting and said,

"What are we accomplishing? This man is performing many miracles. If we let him continue, everyone will believe in him, and the Romans will come and take away both our temple and our nation."

One of them, named Caiaphas, was high priest that year. "You know nothing!" he told them. "You don't see that it's necessary for one man to die for the people so the whole nation won't be destroyed." He did not say this on his own, but as high priest that year he was prophesying that Jesus would die on behalf of the nation—and not for the nation only, but that he might gather together all of God's children who had been scattered all over the world.

From that day on they discussed how they might kill him. That is why Jesus stopped walking around openly among the Jews and instead left and went to the town of Ephraim, in the region near the desert. There he stayed with his disciples.

Jesus left that place and was walking along the road when a certain official came running up to him and knelt down. "Good teacher," he asked Jesus, "what good thing should I do to inherit eternal life?"

"Why do you call me 'good'?" Jesus answered. "No one is good except God only. But if you want to gain life, obey the commandments."

"Which ones?" the man replied.

"You know the commandments," Jesus said: "'Do not commit adultery, do not murder, do not steal, do not lie, do not cheat, honor your father and your mother, love your neighbor as yourself.'"

The young man answered, "Teacher, I have kept all of these since I was a boy. What do I still lack?"

When Jesus heard him say these things, he loved him, and he fixed his eyes on him and said, "You still lack one thing. If you want to lack nothing, then go, sell everything you have and give it to the poor, and you will have treasure in heaven. Then come, take up the cross and follow me."

When the young man heard this he sadly went away, because he was very wealthy.

Seeing his sadness, Jesus turned and said to the disciples, "I tell you the truth, how hard it is for a rich person to enter the kingdom of God!"

The disciples were astonished at this, but Jesus said, "Children, how hard it is to enter the kingdom of God! I tell you again, it's easier for a camel to pass through the eye of a (sewing) needle than for a rich person to enter the kingdom of God."

When they heard this, they were astonished and said to one another, "Then who can be saved?"

Jesus fixed his eyes on them and said, "This is impossible for people, but not with God. All things are possible with God."

Then Peter began saying to him, "Look how we have left everything and have followed you. What will there be in this for us?"

"I tell you the truth," Jesus answered, "at the renewal of all things when the Son of Man sits on the throne of his glory, all you who have followed me will sit on twelve thrones and judge the twelve tribes of Israel."

He said to them, "I tell you the truth, no one has ever left house or parents or brothers or sisters or wife or children or property for the sake of my name and the sake of the good news and the kingdom of God, who will not receive in this age a hundred times as much—houses and brothers and sisters and mothers and children and property—and persecution. And in the age to come, you will inherit eternal life.

"Still, many who are now first will be last, and those who are last will be first.

"For the kingdom of heaven is like the master of a house who went out early in the morning to hire workers for his vineyard. He agreed to pay the workers one denarius for the day's work and sent them into his vineyard.

"When he went out about nine o'clock, he saw some other men standing idle in the marketplace. 'You, too, go to work in my vineyard,' he told them, 'and I'll pay you whatever is right.' So they went to work as well. The master did the same thing around noon and again at three o'clock.

"About five o'clock he went out and found others standing around. 'Why do you stand here idle all day?' he said. 'Because no one hired us,' they answered. He replied, 'You, too, report to my vineyard, and I'll pay you whatever is right.'

"When evening came, the vineyard owner said to his foreman, 'Call in the workers and pay them, starting with the last ones hired and working on up to the first ones.' When those who were hired around five o'clock came, they each received a denarius. When the first to be hired came to be paid, they each thought they would receive more than this. But each one was paid a denarius.

"So they complained to the owner. 'These last men worked only one hour, yet you paid them the same amount as those of us who were out there laboring during the hottest part of the day!'

"But the owner replied, 'My friend, I'm not treating you unfairly. Didn't you agree to work for a denarius? So take your payment and go home. I intentionally paid those men the same amount I paid you. Don't I have the right to do what I want with my money? Or are you envious because I'm generous?'

"In just this way, the last will be first, and the first will be last."

As they walked on the road on their way to Jerusalem, Jesus led the way while the disciples followed in fear and astonishment. Then he took the twelve aside and began to tell them what was about to happen to him.

"We are going up to Jerusalem," he said, "and everything the prophets have written about the Son of Man will come true. He will be betrayed to the chief priests and the teachers of the law, and they will condemn him to death and hand him over to the Gentiles to be crucified. He will be mocked and treated shamelessly and spat upon, and they will flog him and execute him. But on the third day he will rise again."

They understood nothing of what he told them, however. The meaning was hidden from them, and they could not comprehend what he was saying.

Then the mother of James and John (Zebedee's sons) came to Jesus with her sons and knelt in front of him. "Teacher," they said, "we want you to do for us whatever we ask."

"What do you want me to do for you?" he said.

Their mother replied, "Grant that my two sons may sit with you in the glory of your kingdom, one at your right hand and the other at your left."

"You don't know what you're asking," Jesus answered them. "Are you able to drink the cup I will drink, and to be baptized with the baptism I will undergo?"

"Yes," they replied, "we are able."

"You will certainly drink the cup I drink," Jesus told them, "and be baptized with the baptism I undergo. But I don't have the right to grant anyone the privilege of sitting at my right or left. Those places belong to the ones for whom my Father has prepared them."

When the other ten heard what had happened, they were indignant at James and John. But Jesus called them together and said, "You know that the rulers of the nations lord it over their subjects, and their 'great' ones domineer over them. Yet it isn't to be that way among you. If any of you wants to be great, then let him become a servant. And whoever wants to be first among you must become the slave of everyone—just as the Son of Man came not to be served but to serve, and to give his life as a ransom for many!"

As Jesus was nearing Jericho, a blind man was sitting by the roadside, begging. When he heard the crowd passing by, he asked what was going on. They told him, "Jesus of Nazareth is passing by."

"Jesus, Son of David!" he shouted. "Have pity on me!"

Those walking in front began to rebuke him, telling him to be quiet. This only made him shout all the more, "Son of David, have pity on me!"

Jesus stopped and ordered that he be brought to him. As the man came near, Jesus asked him, "What do you want me to do for you?"

"Lord, I want to see!" he replied.

Jesus was moved with compassion. "Receive your sight," he said. "Your faith has healed you." Then Jesus touched the man's eyes, and he immediately received sight and followed him, giving glory to God. Everyone who saw what happened praised God.

Then they reached Jericho. As Jesus entered the city and began passing through it, a rich man named Zacchaeus, one of the chief tax collectors, appeared. He wanted to see who Jesus was, but since he was too short to see over the crowds, he ran ahead and climbed a sycamore tree along the route Jesus was traveling.

When Jesus reached the spot, he looked up and saw him and said, "Zacchaeus, come down quickly because I must visit your home today." So he quickly climbed down and welcomed Jesus with joy.

They all grumbled about this when they saw it. "He has gone to stay with a man who is a sinner," they said.

Zacchaeus was standing there, and he said, "Lord, I'll give half of everything I own to the poor, and whatever I may have extorted from anyone I'll pay back four times as much."

"Salvation has come to this home today," Jesus said, "because this man, too, is a descendant of Abraham. The Son of Man came to seek and to save those who were lost."

As the people were listening to him, Jesus told this parable since he was nearing Jerusalem, and they thought the kingdom of God would soon appear:

"A nobleman traveled to a distant country to be crowned king, planning to return afterward. He summoned ten of his servants and gave each of them an amount equal to three months' wages. 'Conduct business until I return,' he told them. But his citizens hated him and sent a delegation to follow him. 'We don't want this man to rule over us!' they said.

"After the nobleman was crowned king and returned home, he ordered his ten servants who had been given the money to appear before him so he could find out how well each of them had done. The first came forward and said, 'Sir, your money has earned ten times as much.' The king replied, 'Well done, good servant! Since you were faithful in a thing of little importance, you will take charge of ten cities.'

"Then the second man came forward and said, 'Sir, your money has earned five times as much.' In the same way the nobleman answered him, 'You will take charge of five cities.'

"Then another man stepped forward and said, 'Sir, here is your money, which I hid in a piece of cloth. I did this because I was afraid of you. You're a harsh man. You take out what you didn't put in, and you reap what you didn't sow.'

"The king said to this man, 'I'll judge you by the words of your own mouth, you wicked servant! So you knew I'm a harsh man, who takes out what I didn't put in and who reaps what I didn't sow? Then why didn't you put my money in the bank so I could at least earn interest?'

"Then he ordered those who were standing by, 'Take the money from him and give it to the man who multiplied his money tenfold.'

"'Sir,' they replied, 'he already has ten times as much!'

"And he answered, 'I'm telling you that whoever has will be given more, but whoever does not have will lose even what little he has. And as for those enemies of mine who didn't want me to rule over them, bring them here and execute them in front of me.'"

After saying these things, Jesus walked on ahead of them toward Jerusalem. A large crowd was following as he and his disciples left Jericho. By the roadside sat a blind man named Bartimaeus (son of Timaeus), who was begging. When he heard that Jesus of Nazareth was passing by, he began to shout, "Lord, Jesus, Son of David, have pity on me!"

Many people told him to be quiet, but he shouted even more, "Son of David, have pity on me!"

Jesus stopped and ordered the man to be brought to him. So they called the blind man and said to him, "Take courage! Get up, he's calling you." He threw off his cloak, got up, and came to Jesus.

Then Jesus said to him, "What do you want me to do for you?"

"Dear rabbi," said Bartimaeus, "let me see again."

Jesus was moved with compassion, touched his eyes, and said to him, "Go home; your faith has healed you." Immediately he could see, and he followed Jesus on the road, glorifying God.

ೲ

THE LAST WEEK
OF MINISTRY

Passover Week AD 33

The Jews' Feast of Unleavened Bread, called the Passover, was approaching, and many left the country and headed to Jerusalem to purify themselves before the Passover arrived. They were looking for Jesus there, and as they stood in the temple, they kept discussing with each other, "Do you think he'll come to the feast, or not?"

The chief priests and the Pharisees had ordered anyone knowing his whereabouts to report it to them because they intended to arrest him.

Six days before the Passover Jesus came to Bethany, where Lazarus lived (the man whom Jesus raised from the dead). There at Bethany they prepared dinner for him at the home of Simon the leper. Martha was serving, and Lazarus was one of those eating with him.

Then Mary took an alabaster jar of expensive ointment (a pound of pure nard) and came up to him as he reclined at the table. She broke the jar and poured the ointment over his head. She anointed his feet and wiped his feet with her hair. The house soon was filled with the aroma of the ointment.

When his disciples saw what she did, some became indignant and said to themselves, "Why is this ointment being wasted? This could have been sold for a considerable amount of money." So they began to rebuke her. Judas Iscariot (who would later betray him) said, "Why wasn't this ointment sold for a year's wages, and the money given to the poor?" He didn't say this because he was at all concerned about the poor but because he was a thief and had charge of the money pouch and kept stealing what was put into it.

Jesus was aware of all this and said to them, "Leave her alone. Why are you bothering the woman? She has done a good thing for me. She has saved this ointment for the day of my burial. You always have the poor with you and can help them whenever you want, but you won't always have me. She has done what she could. In pouring out this ointment she has anointed my body for burial. I tell you the truth, wherever in the world this good news is proclaimed, what this woman has done will also be recounted in memory of her."

Many of the Jews who knew he was there came not only because of Jesus but because they wanted to see Lazarus, whom Jesus had raised from the dead. That is why the chief priests discussed how they might also kill Lazarus. On account of him a large number of Jews were leaving them and believing in Jesus.

When they approached Jerusalem the next day and came to Bethphage on the Mount of Olives, Jesus sent out two of his disciples. "Go into the village ahead of you. As soon as you enter it, you will find a donkey tied up. Tied with her will be a colt which no one has ever ridden. Untie them and bring them to me. If anyone says anything or asks, 'What are you doing?' say to him, 'The Lord needs them,' and he'll immediately send them here."

Those who were sent left and did what Jesus told them. They found a young donkey tied outside the door in the street just as he had described, and they untied it.

The owners were standing there and said, "What are you doing? Why are you untying the colt?"

"The Lord needs it," they said, repeating what Jesus had told them to say.

Then the owners let them go. So they brought the donkey and the colt to Jesus, threw their clothing on them, and sat Jesus on the colt.

As he rode along, they began to spread their articles of clothing on the road. When he came to the place where the road goes down the Mount of Olives, a large crowd of disciples began to shout for joy and to praise God loudly for all the miracles they had seen. "Blessed is the King who is coming in the name of the Lord!" they shouted. "Peace in heaven, and glory in the highest!"

A huge crowd had come to the feast. When they heard that Jesus was entering Jerusalem, they cut down palm branches, went out to meet him, and spread the branches on the road. The crowds who followed him as well as those who went ahead of him kept shouting, "Hosanna! Hosanna to the Son of David!" "Blessed is he who is coming in the name of the Lord, the king of Israel!" "Blessed is the kingdom of our father David!" "Hosanna in the highest!"

All this happened to fulfill what the prophet said:

> *"Tell the daughter of Zion,*
> *'Don't be afraid! Look,*
> *your king is coming to you,*
> *humble, and riding a donkey,*
> *even a colt, the foal of a donkey.'"*

The disciples didn't understand these things at first. But after Jesus was glorified, they remembered these predictions about him and that they had done these things to him.

The people who were with him when he raised Lazarus from the dead and called him from the tomb were telling others all about it. That is why the people went out to meet him; they heard that he had performed this great miracle.

Some Pharisees in the crowd said to him, "Teacher, restrain your disciples."

But he answered them, "I'm telling you, if they were to keep quiet, the very stones would cry out!"

When he came near and saw the city, he wept over it. "If only you—yes, you—had known on this special day the things that would bring you peace! But now they are hidden from you. The days are coming when your enemies will build a siege ramp around you and encircle you and hem you in on all sides. They will level you to the ground—with your children inside you—and will not leave one stone upon another. This will happen because you didn't recognize the time of God's coming to you."

The whole city was aroused when he entered Jerusalem. "Who is this?" they asked.

The crowds answered, "This is Jesus the prophet, from Nazareth in Galilee."

Then the Pharisees said to each other, "See, we are accomplishing nothing. Look at how the whole world has gone after him!"

Jesus entered the temple, and when he had looked around at everything, he left for Bethany with the twelve since it was already quite late.

As Jesus was returning to Jerusalem from Bethany the next morning, he became hungry. In the distance by the side of the road he saw a fig tree covered with leaves, so he went to find fruit on it. When he reached it, he found only the leaves (it wasn't the right season for figs). So Jesus said to it, "May you bear no fruit from this time onward, and may no one ever eat your fruit again!"

His disciples heard him say it. And the fig tree immediately withered.

Then they came to Jerusalem, and Jesus went into the temple of God and began to drive out everyone who was selling and buying things there. He overturned the tables of the money changers and the chairs of those selling doves and would not allow anyone to carry merchandise through the temple. He began to teach them, "Doesn't Scripture say, 'My house will be called a house of prayer for all the nations'? But you have made it a den of robbers!"

The Buyers and Sellers Driven Out of the Temple

The chief priests and the teachers of the law heard what had happened, and continued to seek a way to kill him. They were afraid of him because all the people marveled at his teaching.

The blind and the lame came to him in the temple, and he healed them. But when the chief priests and the teachers of the law saw the wonderful things he was doing and heard the children shouting in the temple, "Hosanna to the Son of David!" they became furious. They said to him, "Do you hear what they're saying?"

"Yes!" Jesus replied. "Have you never read, 'From the mouths of babes and infants you have ordained praise'?"

Then he left them, and when evening came, he left the city and spent the night in Bethany.

The next morning they passed by the fig tree and saw that it had dried up from the roots. Peter remembered and said to Jesus, "Master, look! The fig tree you cursed has shriveled up."

When the disciples saw it, they were bewildered. "How did the fig tree dry up so quickly?" they said.

"Have faith in God," Jesus answered. "I tell you the truth, if you have faith and don't doubt, you will do far more than what was done to the fig tree. Whoever says to this mountain, 'Throw yourself into the sea,' and doesn't doubt in the least that it will take place, that person will receive whatever he says. I'm telling you that whatever you ask for in prayer—as long as you truly believe you will receive it—it will be yours.

"As you stand and pray, if you have anything against someone, forgive. Then your heavenly Father will also forgive you your offenses. But if you do not forgive, neither will your Father in heaven forgive your offenses."

So they returned to Jerusalem. As Jesus was walking in the temple, teaching the people and announcing the good news, the chief priests, teachers of the law, and elders of the people approached him and said, "Tell us by what authority you are doing these things. Who gave you such authority?"

"Let me ask you a question first," Jesus said. "Answer me, and I'll tell you by what authority I'm doing these things. The baptism of John—did it come from heaven or from men? Answer me!"

They discussed it with each other and said, "If we say, 'From heaven,' he'll say to us, 'Then why didn't you believe him?' But if we say, 'From men,' we are afraid of this crowd. The people will stone us because they're convinced John was truly a prophet."

So they replied to Jesus, "We don't know."

Jesus answered them, "Then neither will I tell you by what authority I'm doing these things."

Jesus began to speak to them in parables: "What do you think? A man had two sons. He came to the first and said, 'Son, go work in my vineyard today.' His son replied, 'I won't.' But afterward he changed his mind and went. Then the man came to his second son and said the same thing to him. This son replied, 'I'll go, sir,' but he didn't. Which of the two sons obeyed his father?"

They replied, "The first one."

"I tell you the truth," Jesus said, "the tax collectors and prostitutes will make it into the kingdom of God before you will. John came to show you the way of righteousness, and though you didn't believe him, the tax collectors and prostitutes did. Even when you saw this, however, you didn't change your minds and believe him."

Every day he was teaching in the temple. The chief priests and the teachers of the law and the leaders of the people kept looking for ways to kill him, but they couldn't find a way to do it because the people were hanging on his words.

Then he began to tell the people, "Listen to another parable. The master of a house planted a vineyard and put up a fence around it, dug out a winepress, and built a tower. Then he leased it out to vine growers and left the country for a long time. When harvest time approached, he sent a servant to the vine growers to collect his fruit. But the vine growers beat the servant and sent him away without any fruit.

"Then he sent them another servant, but this one they beat and stoned and gashed his head. After tormenting him, they sent him away without any fruit. The master sent a third servant, and they wounded him and threw him out as well.

"Again he sent many others, and they did the same things to them—beating some and killing others.

"The owner of the vineyard said, 'What should I do?' He had an only son, whom he dearly loved, and at last he sent him. 'I'll send my dearly loved son,' he said. 'Perhaps they will respect my son when they see him.' But when the vine growers saw the son, they plotted with each other and said, 'This is the heir! Let's kill him so the inheritance will be ours.' So they seized him, threw him out of the vineyard, and killed him.

"So then, when the owner of the vineyard comes, what will he do to those vine growers?"

They replied, "He'll put those wicked men to an agonizing death and then will lease out the vineyard to other vine growers who will pay him his share of the crop at harvest time."

Jesus said to them, "He will come and kill those vine growers and then give the vineyard to others! I'm telling you, in the same way the kingdom of God will be taken from you and will be given to a people who will produce its fruit."

When they heard this they said, "May it never happen!"

But he fixed his eyes on them and said, "Then what does this Scripture mean? Have you never read where it says,

> *'The stone the builders rejected*
> *has become the capstone.*
> *The Lord himself did this*
> *and it is marvelous in our eyes'?*

"Whoever falls on this stone will be destroyed, and whoever the stone falls on will be crushed into powder!"

When the chief priests and the teachers of the law and the Pharisees heard these parables, they knew Jesus was speaking about them. Immediately they tried to arrest him, but because they were afraid of the people who considered him a prophet, they left him alone and went away.

Once more Jesus spoke to them in parables: "The kingdom of heaven is like a king who prepared a wedding banquet for his son. He sent out his servants to call those who had been invited to the banquet, but they refused to come.

"So he sent out other servants and instructed them to tell those who had been invited, 'See here, my dinner has been prepared. The oxen and the fattened cattle have been butchered, and everything is ready. Come to the wedding banquet!' But they made light of it and went their separate ways, one to his farm, another to his business. The others grabbed his servants, insulted them, then killed them.

"When the king heard this he was furious. He sent troops to destroy those murderers and burn down their city. Then he said to his servants, 'The wedding banquet is ready to begin, but those who were invited did not deserve to come. So go out to the main thoroughfares and invite anyone you find to come to the wedding banquet.' The servants went out to the main thoroughfares and gathered everyone they found, both good and evil people. Then the wedding hall was filled up with guests.

"But when the king came in to see his guests, he saw one man there who wasn't wearing wedding clothes. He said to him, 'My friend, how did you get in here without wedding clothes?' The man was speechless. Then the king said to his servants, 'Tie him up hand and foot, and throw him out into the darkness, where people are weeping and gnashing their teeth.'

"For many are called, but few are chosen."

At that time the Pharisees plotted how they might be able to trap Jesus in what he said. They watched him and sent out spies who pretended to be sincere in order to catch him in some criminal statement so as to hand him over to the power and authority of the governor.

So they sent to him some of their disciples and a few Herodians to trap him with a question. "Teacher," they said, "we know you are truthful and that you speak and teach rightly and are not partial to anyone. You pay no regard to how prominent men might be, but instead teach truthfully the way of God. So tell us: In your opinion, is it legal for us to give tribute to Caesar or not? Should we give it or not?"

Jesus knew their hypocrisy and cunning and wickedness. He said to them, "Why are you trying to trick me, you hypocrites? Show me the tribute money. Let me see a denarius."

So they brought him the coin. "Whose image and inscription is this?" he asked them.

They answered, "Caesar's."

"Give to Caesar what belongs to Caesar," Jesus said to them, "and give to God what belongs to God."

So they were unable to trap him in his words in front of the people. Stunned by his answer, they became silent, then left him and went away.

That day some of the Sadducees (who say there is no resurrection) came to him with a question. "Teacher," they said, "Moses told us that if a man dies without leaving children, his brother is to marry the widow and produce children for his brother.

"Now there were seven brothers with us. The first married a woman and died without having children. So the second married her but also died childless. Then the third one married her and so on for all seven brothers, all dying without having children. Finally the woman died as well. So in the resurrection when they all rise, whose wife will she be? All seven had married her!"

"You're wrong," Jesus replied, "because you don't understand the Scriptures—or the power of God. People in this world get married and are given in marriage, but those who are considered worthy to take part in the next world and the resurrection from the dead neither get married nor are given in marriage. Instead, they are like the angels in heaven. They cannot die anymore, either, because they're like the angels and are children of God since they participated in the resurrection.

"Now concerning the resurrection of the dead— even Moses indicated that the dead will be raised. Haven't you read what God said in the book of Moses, in the story of the bush, when he called the Lord 'the

God of Abraham and the God of Isaac and the God of Jacob'? He isn't the God of the dead but of the living. Everyone is alive to him! That is why you have made an enormous mistake."

When the crowds heard his teaching they were astonished. Even some of the teachers of the law said to him, "Well said, teacher!" From then on none of them dared to ask him anything.

When the Pharisees heard that Jesus had silenced the Sadducees, they called a meeting. One of them, an expert among the teachers of the law, had witnessed these encounters and knew Jesus had answered well. So he came up to Jesus and tested him with this question: "Teacher, what is the greatest of all the commandments? Which is the first commandment of all?"

Jesus answered, "The first of all the commandments is this: 'Hear, O Israel! The Lord our God is one Lord, and you shall love the Lord your God with all your heart and with all your soul and with all your mind and with all your strength.' This is the first and greatest commandment. The second is like it: 'You shall love your neighbor as yourself.' The whole law and all the prophets depend on these two commandments. There is no commandment greater than these two."

"Teacher, you have spoken the truth," replied the expert on the law. "There is only one God, and to love him with all your heart and understanding and strength—and to love your neighbor as much as you do yourself—is worth more than all burnt offerings and sacrifices."

When Jesus saw that he gave a wise answer, he said to him, "You aren't far from the kingdom of God."

When the Pharisees were together while Jesus was teaching in the temple, he asked them a question: "What do you think about the Messiah? Whose Son is he?"

"The Son of David," they said.

So he replied, "If the teachers of the law say the Messiah is David's son, then how can David through the Spirit call him 'Lord'? David himself said through the Holy Spirit in the book of Psalms, 'The Lord said to my Lord, "Sit by my right hand, until I make your enemies your footstool."'"

"David himself clearly calls him 'Lord.' So how can he be his son?"

No one could answer him a word, and from then on no one dared to ask him another question. Yet the large crowd of ordinary people listened to him eagerly. Day after day he was teaching in the temple, while each night he left to stay on the Mount of Olives.

All the people kept coming to Jesus early in the morning to hear him speak. Then he taught his disciples so everyone could hear:

"Be careful and watch out for the teachers of the law! They like to walk around in long robes and love to sit in the places of honor at banquets and in the best seats in the synagogues. They consume widows' houses and say long prayers to make a show. Their condemnations will be severe!

"The teachers of the law and the Pharisees sit in Moses' seat. That is why you should observe and do everything they tell you to. But don't copy the way they live! They don't do what they teach.

"They lay burdens on people that are heavy and hard to carry. Yet they won't lift a finger to help them. Everything they do, they do to be noticed. They create big phylacteries and make long tassels on their prayer shawls. They love to strut in dignified robes in the market places with people calling them, 'Rabbi, [Rabbi].'

"As for you, don't let yourselves be called 'Rabbi.' You have only one teacher, the Christ, and you are all brothers. And don't call anyone on earth your father because you have only one Father, the one who is in heaven. Don't call yourselves 'masters,' either. You have only one master, the Christ. Whoever is the greatest among you must be your servant. And whoever elevates himself will be humbled, while whoever humbles himself will be elevated.

"[Destruction awaits you, teachers of the law and Pharisees—hypocrites! You keep people out of the kingdom of heaven. You don't enter it yourselves, and you prevent others who want to go in from doing so.]

"Destruction awaits you, teachers of the law and Pharisees—hypocrites! You devour widows' houses, covering your evil with long prayers; therefore you shall receive greater condemnation.

"Destruction awaits you, teachers of the law and Pharisees—hypocrites! You travel over sea and land to make a single convert, and when he has been won, you make him twice as much a son of hell as yourselves.

"Destruction awaits you, you blind guides who say, 'If anyone takes an oath by the temple, it is nothing, but if anyone takes an oath by the gold of the temple, he must make good his oath.' You're blind and foolish! Which is greater—the gold, or the temple which makes the gold holy?

"You also say, 'If anyone takes an oath by the altar, it is nothing, but if anyone takes an oath by the gift on the altar, he must make good his oath.' You're blind and foolish! Which is greater—the gift or the altar which makes the gift holy?

"Whoever takes an oath by the altar swears by it and by everything on it. And whoever takes an oath by the temple swears by it and by the one who lives in it. And whoever takes an oath by heaven swears by the throne of God and by the one who sits on it.

"Destruction awaits you, teachers of the law and Pharisees—hypocrites! You give God a tenth of your mint and dill and cumin but have ignored the more important things in the law—justice, mercy, and faithfulness. You should have done the former without neglecting the latter, you blind guides who strain out a gnat but swallow a camel!

"Destruction awaits you, teachers of the law and Pharisees—hypocrites! You wash the outside of the cup and the dish, but inside they are full of robbery and self-indulgence. You blind Pharisee, first wash the inside of the cup and the dish. Then the outside can be clean as well.

"Destruction awaits you, teachers of the law and Pharisees—hypocrites! You're like whitewashed tombs that look beautiful on the outside, but inside are full of dead men's bones and all kinds of filth. In the same way, on the outside you look quite godly to men, but on the inside you're full of hypocrisy and sin.

"Destruction awaits you, teachers of the law and Pharisees—hypocrites! You build the tombs of the prophets and decorate the graves of the godly and say, 'If we had lived in the days of our ancestors, we wouldn't have joined them in killing the prophets.'

In this way you testify that you're the descendants of those who murdered the prophets. So fill up what your ancestors are accountable for!

"You snakes, you children of vipers! How will you escape being sentenced to hell? Because of this, understand that I will send you prophets and wise men and teachers of the law, some of whom you will kill and crucify, while others you will flog in your synagogues and persecute from city to city. Then all the righteous blood that has been spilled on the earth from that of righteous Abel to the blood of Zechariah, the son of Berekiah—whom you killed between the sanctuary and the altar—will be laid to your account. I tell you the truth, all this will happen to this generation of people.

"O Jerusalem, Jerusalem! You have killed the prophets and stoned those who were sent to you! How often I would have gathered your children, as a hen gathers her brood under her wings—and you refused! Look! Your house will be left desolate. I tell you the truth, you will not see me anymore until you say, 'Blessed is the one who comes in the name of the Lord!'"

Across from the treasury, Jesus sat down and watched how the people were dropping money into the chest. Many rich people put in large amounts. But he looked up and also saw a poor widow putting in two tiny copper coins which amount to less than a cent.

The Widow's Mite

Calling his disciples together, he said to them, "I tell you, this poor widow put in more than all who contributed to the treasury. They all gave to God out of their wealth. But she in her poverty put in everything she had to live on."

Some Greeks who had come up to worship at the feast approached Philip (the one from Bethsaida in Galilee) and asked him, "Sir, we would like to see Jesus." Philip went to tell Andrew, and the two of them told Jesus.

But Jesus answered, "The time has come for the Son of Man to be glorified. I tell you the truth, unless a kernel of wheat falls into the ground and dies, it remains by itself. But if it dies, it bears much fruit. Whoever loves his life will lose it, but whoever hates his life in this world will keep it to life eternal.

"If anyone serves me, let him follow me. Where I am, there my servant will be as well. And the Father will honor anyone who serves me.

"Now I am greatly distressed. And what should I say? 'Father, save me from this time'? No! This is the very reason I have come to this time. Father, glorify your name!"

At that moment a voice from heaven said, "I have glorified it already, and I will glorify it again."

The crowds standing by who heard this said that it had thundered. Others said, "An angel has spoken to him."

Jesus said, "This voice did not come for my sake but for yours. The time for the condemnation of the world has arrived. Now the ruler of this world will be cast out! And when I am lifted up from earth, I will draw everyone to myself." He said this to describe the kind of death he would undergo.

The people answered, "We have heard that the law says the Messiah will live forever. Then how can you say the Son of Man must be lifted up? Who is this Son of Man?"

"The light is with you for only a little while longer," Jesus replied. "Walk while you still have the light so the darkness will not overtake you. No one who walks in the dark knows where he is going. Put your trust in the light while you have the light; in that way you will become children of light."

After Jesus said these things, he left and hid from them. Even though he had done so many miracles right in front of them, they didn't believe in him. In that way the word of the prophet Isaiah was fulfilled:

"Lord, who has believed our report?

And to whom has the power of the Lord been revealed?"

This is why they couldn't believe. As Isaiah also said:

> *"He has blinded their eyes and hardened their heart,*
> *otherwise they would see with their eyes*
> *and understand with their heart*
> *and turn around, and I would heal them."*

Isaiah said these things because he saw Jesus' glory and spoke about him.

Still, there were many even among the rulers who did believe in him. For fear of the Pharisees, however, they didn't admit it publicly lest they be thrown out of the synagogue. For they loved the approval of men more than the approval of God.

Then Jesus said in a loud voice, "Whoever believes in me does not believe only in me, but in the one who sent me. Whoever sees me sees the one who sent me. I have come into the world as a light so that whoever believes in me will not remain in the dark.

"If someone hears what I say and doesn't believe, I am not his judge. I didn't come to judge the world but to save the world. The one who rejects me and dismisses what I say has another judge. The word I spoke will judge him on the last day.

"I didn't speak on my own authority, but the Father who sent me is the one who commanded me what to say and speak. I know his command gives eternal life. I am speaking only what the Father told me to say."

As Jesus was leaving the temple, his disciples began to point out to him its structures that were richly decorated with precious stones and consecrated gifts. One of his disciples exclaimed, "See, master, what tremendous stones and what fabulous buildings!"

"Are you looking at these impressive buildings?" Jesus said. "I tell you the truth, the days are coming when not a single stone of these buildings you admire will be left upon another. They will all be thrown down!"

Later, as Jesus sat on the Mount of Olives across from the temple, Peter, James, John, and Andrew came to him privately and asked, "Teacher, please tell us— when will all these things happen? What will be the sign when all these things are about to take place? And what sign will proclaim your coming and the end of the age?"

Then Jesus began to tell them, "Watch out so no one misleads you. Many will come in my name and say, 'I am he,' 'I am the Messiah,' and 'The time is getting close.' They will deceive many people. Make sure you don't follow them!

"You will hear about wars and rumors of wars, but when you hear such reports, don't be terrified, and see to it you aren't disturbed. All these things must take place first, but the end will not come immediately.

"Nation will rise against nation and kingdom against kingdom, and there will be famines and epidemics and great earthquakes all over the world. But even this is only the beginning of the agony. There will be frightening sights and great signs in the sky.

Watch out! Beware of others, because before these things take place, they will hand you over to be tortured and will put you to death. They will arrest you and persecute you, handing you over to the synagogues and to ruling councils and to prison. They will whip you in their synagogues, and you will be dragged in front of governors and kings because of me. Yet this will give you an opportunity to testify before them and the Gentiles.

"When they hand you over and lead you away and bring you before the synagogues and the rulers and authorities, don't worry beforehand about how or what you should say in your defense. You are to say whatever you are given at that moment. The Holy Spirit will teach you what to say. It isn't you who will be speaking but the Spirit of the Father who speaks in you. So settle it in your heart not to ponder beforehand what you should say. I will give you words and wisdom that none of your adversaries will be able to answer or refute.

"You will be hated by everyone for the sake of my name. Many will be led into sin and will betray one another and hate each other. Brother will hand over brother to death, and a father will do the same to his child. Children will rebel against their parents and put them to death. You will be betrayed even by parents and brothers and relatives and friends. Some of you they will kill, and you will be hated by everyone for the sake of my name. Yet you will not lose even a single hair on your head. Through patient endurance you will gain your souls.

"When you see Jerusalem encircled by armies, then realize that the time for her destruction has arrived. Those who are in Judea should flee to the mountains; those who are in the city should run out of it, and those who are in the country should not enter the city. Those are the days of vengeance, when everything that has been written will be fulfilled.

"How hard those days will be for pregnant women and those who are nursing! There will be great distress throughout the land and upon this people. They will be killed by the sword and will be led captive to all the nations. Jerusalem will be trampled by the Gentiles until the times of the Gentiles are fulfilled.

"Many false prophets will appear and will deceive many people. Because evil will run rampant, the love of many will grow cold. But whoever endures to the end will be saved.

"When they persecute you in this city, flee to the next. I tell you the truth, you will not have visited every city in Israel before the Son of Man comes.

"This good news of the kingdom must first be preached all over the world as a testimony to all the nations. Then the end will come.

"When you see the abomination that makes desolation, predicted by Daniel the prophet, standing in the holy place where it shouldn't be" (let the reader understand), "then those in Judea should flee to the mountains! A man on the housetop should not go down into the house or go inside to take anything out. And the man in the field shouldn't return to get his clothes.

"How terrible those days will be for pregnant women and those who are nursing! Pray that your escape will not be in winter or on the Sabbath. At that time there will be a great tribulation, the likes of which has never occurred from the creation of the world until now and will never happen again.

"If the Lord had not shortened those days, none of humankind would survive. But for the sake of God's chosen people, those days will be shortened.

"If anyone says to you at that time, 'Look, here's the Messiah!' or 'Look, he's there!' don't believe it. False messiahs and false prophets will appear and perform such impressive signs and miracles that, if it were possible, even God's chosen people would be misled. So don't forget! See, I've told you everything beforehand.

"If someone says to you, 'Look, he's in the desert,' don't go out there. Or, 'Look, he's in the private rooms,' don't believe them. In the same way that lightning comes from the East and shines as far as the West, so will the Son of Man come. The vultures gather wherever the corpse lies.

"Immediately after the tribulation of those days, signs will appear in the sun and the moon and the stars. The sun will be darkened, the moon will not shine, and the stars will fall from the sky. And on earth the nations will be frantic and perplexed. The sea and its waves will be roaring, and people's hearts will give out because of fear about the things that are coming on the world.

"The powers of the heavens will be shaken. And then the sign of the Son of Man will appear in the sky. At that time all the nations of the earth will mourn as they see the Son of Man coming on the clouds of heaven with power and great glory. Then with a loud trumpet call he will send out his angels to gather his chosen people from the four winds—from the farthest part of earth to the farthest part of heaven and from one end of heaven to the other.

"When you see these things beginning to take place, lift your heads and look up because your redemption is drawing near."

Then he told them a parable: "Learn a lesson from the fig tree. Observe it and all the trees. When you see its branches send out shoots and leaves start to appear, you know summer is near. In the same way, when you see all these things taking place, know that the kingdom of God is drawing near—even at the door! I tell you the truth, this generation will by no means pass away before all these things will have been fulfilled. Heaven and earth will pass away, but my words will not pass away!

"Yet no one knows exactly when this will happen, including the angels of heaven and the Son; only my Father knows. The events of Noah's day give a good picture of what the coming of the Son of Man will be like. In the days before the flood, people were eating and drinking, getting married and being given in marriage, until the day Noah entered the ark. They were unaware of what was happening until the flood came and swept them all away. The coming of the Son of Man will be like that. Two men will be in the field; one will be taken and the other will be left. Two women will be grinding grain at the mill; one will be taken and the other left.

"So watch yourselves and make sure your hearts do not become weighed down by wild living and drunkenness and the worries of this life. Then that day would surprise you. It will come like a trap on everyone living on the face of the earth! That is why you should continually watch and pray that you may have strength to escape all these things that are certain to come about, and to stand before the Son of Man. Therefore, be careful! Keep watch because you don't know when your Lord is coming.

"It's like a man who took a trip abroad. He left his home after putting his servants in charge, giving each of them something to do. And he ordered his doorkeeper to watch carefully. You too should watch because you don't know when the master of the house will return—whether in the evening, at midnight, at dawn, or in the morning. Whenever he comes, don't let him find you asleep! I'm saying this not only to you but to everybody: Watch!

"The kingdom of heaven could be compared at that time to ten young girls who took their lamps and went out to meet the bridegroom. Five of them were wise, and five were foolish. The foolish ones failed to take along extra oil for their lamps, but the wise ones carried oil in containers along with their lamps.

"When the bridegroom didn't come for a long time, they all dozed off. In the middle of the night the shout went up, 'Look, the bridegroom is coming! Go out to meet him.' Then all the girls got up and lit their lamps. The foolish girls said to the wise, 'Give us some of your oil because our lamps are going out.' But the wise girls answered, 'We can't do that because there wouldn't be enough for both us and you. Instead, go to the store and buy yourselves some oil.'

"While they left to buy some oil, the bridegroom arrived, and those who were prepared joined him at the wedding banquet. Then the door was shut. Some time later the other young girls arrived and said, 'Lord! Lord! Open the door for us!' But he answered them, 'I tell you the truth, I don't know you.'

"That is why you should watch because you do not know exactly when the Son of Man is coming.

"It's like a man taking a trip abroad who called his servants together and put them in charge of his estate. To one man he allocated five portions of his capital, to another two, and to yet another one—each according to his ability. Then he immediately left on his trip.

"The one who was given the five parts went off and earned five more. In a similar way the one with two allotments earned two more. But the one who was given the one portion dug a hole in the ground and buried his master's money.

"After a long time the master of those servants returned to settle accounts with them. The one who had been given the five allotments appeared before him and presented him with the additional five. 'Sir,' he said, 'you entrusted me with five shares. Look, I've used them to earn five more.'

"His master replied, 'You've done well, good and faithful servant! You were faithful with a few things; I'll put you in charge of many things. Come and share my joy!'

"In the same way the one who had been given two allotments came and said, 'Sir, you entrusted me with two shares. Look, I've used them to earn two more.' His master replied, 'You've done well, good and faithful servant! You were faithful with a few things; I'll put you in charge of many things. Come and share my joy!'

"Finally the man who had been given the one allotment came and said, 'Sir, I knew you're a hard man—reaping what you didn't plant and gathering what you didn't scatter. I was afraid, so I went out and hid your money in the ground. Look, here's what belongs to you.'

"His master responded, 'you wicked and lazy servant! You knew I reap where I didn't plant and gather what I didn't scatter? Then you should have deposited my money with the bankers, so when I returned I would at least have earned interest.

"'Now take the money from him and give it to the one who has ten portions, because everyone who has will be given more, and he'll have an abundance. But the one who has nothing will be stripped even of what he has. And as for that worthless servant—throw him outside into the darkness where there will be weeping and gnashing of teeth.'

"When the Son of Man comes in his glory with all the holy angels, he will sit on his glorious throne, and all the nations will be gathered in front of him. He will separate them from each other just as a shepherd separates the sheep from the goats. He will put the sheep on his right hand and the goats on his left.

"Then the king will say to those by his right hand, 'Come, you who are blessed by my Father, inherit the kingdom prepared for you since the foundation of the world. For I was hungry and you gave me food. I was thirsty and you gave me drink. I was a stranger and you made me welcome. I was naked and you clothed me. I was sick and you visited me. I was in prison and you came to me.'

"Then the godly will answer him, 'Lord, when did we see you hungry, and we fed you, or thirsty, and we gave you something to drink? Or when did we see you as a stranger, and we welcomed you? Or naked, and we clothed you? Or when did we see you sick or in prison, and we visited you?'

"Then the king will answer them, 'I tell you the truth, because you did it for one of the least esteemed of my brothers, you did it for me.'

"Then he will also say to those on his left, 'Get away from me, you cursed ones, into the everlasting fire prepared for the devil and his angels. For I was hungry, and you gave me no food. I was thirsty, and you gave me no drink. I was a stranger, and you did not make me welcome, naked, and you did not clothe me, sick and in prison, and you did not visit me.'

"Then they will reply to him, 'Lord, when did we see you hungry or thirsty or a stranger or naked or sick or in prison, and we didn't help you?'

"He will answer them, 'I tell you the truth, because you failed to do it for one of the least esteemed of my brothers, you failed to do it for me.' Then they will go away into eternal punishment, but the godly will go into eternal life."

The Passover and the Feast of Unleavened Bread were two days away. When Jesus was finished saying these things, he told his disciples, "You know the Passover is coming in two days, and then the Son of Man will be handed over to be crucified."

At that time the chief priests and the teachers of the law and the elders of the people assembled in the palace of the high priest, Caiaphas, in order to decide how to arrest Jesus secretly and kill him. They said, "We can't do it during the feast, or the people will cause an uproar." They said this because they were afraid of the people.

Then Satan entered into Judas Iscariot, one of the twelve. He left to consult with the chief priests and the captains about how he might betray Jesus to them. He said to them, "What will you give me if I hand him over to you?"

They were delighted when they heard this and promised to give him money. He agreed, and they gave him thirty pieces of silver.

From then on he looked for an opportune time to betray him, when the crowds were gone.

When the first day of the Feast of Unleavened Bread arrived—the day the Passover lamb had to be killed—the disciples came to Jesus and said, "Where would you like us to go to prepare for you to eat the Passover meal?"

He sent Peter and John, telling them, "Go and prepare the Passover meal for us."

"Where do you want us to prepare it?" they said.

"Go into the city, and there you'll meet a man carrying a pitcher of water," he told them. "Follow him, and whatever home he enters, say to the man of the house, 'The teacher says to you, "My time has come. Where is the guest room at your house for me to eat the Passover with my disciples?"'" He'll show you a large upper room, furnished and ready. That is where you should prepare for us."

His disciples left and went into the city as Jesus had instructed them. There they found everything as he had said it would be, and they prepared the Passover.

When it was evening, Jesus came with the twelve. At the appointed time he reclined at the table with the apostles. He told them, "I have earnestly desired to eat this Passover with you before I suffer. For I tell you, I will not observe it again until it finds fulfillment in the kingdom of God."

Then he took the cup and gave thanks and said, "Take this and divide it among yourselves. For I tell you I will not drink at all from the fruit of the vine until the kingdom of God comes."

Jesus knew before the Feast of Passover arrived that the time had come for him to leave this world and return to the Father. Having loved his own who were in the world, he loved them to the fullest extent.

Even before supper had begun, the devil had put it into the heart of Judas Iscariot, Simon's son, to betray Jesus.

Jesus, knowing the Father had given all things into his hands and that he came from God and was going to God, got up from the supper, took off his outer clothing, and wrapped a towel around his waist. Then he poured water into a basin and began to wash the disciples' feet, wiping them with the towel around his waist.

When he came to Simon Peter, Peter said to him, "Lord, do you intend to wash my feet?"

"You don't yet understand what I am doing," Jesus answered, "but later you will."

"You will never wash my feet!" Peter said.

"If I don't wash you," answered Jesus, "you have no part with me."

"Lord, then wash not only my feet," Simon Peter replied, "but also my hands and my head!"

Jesus responded, "The one who has bathed doesn't need to wash anything except his feet—he is completely clean. And you disciples are clean, although not all of you." (He knew who was going to betray him, and this is why he said, "Not all of you are clean.")

After he had washed their feet, he put on his outer garments and again sat down. "Do you understand what I have done to you?" he said. "You call me 'teacher' and 'Lord,' and you are right; that is exactly who I am. So if I, your Lord and teacher, have washed your feet, you also ought to wash each other's feet. I gave you an example—you should do as I have done to you. I tell you the truth, a servant isn't greater than his master, nor is a messenger greater than the one who sent him. Since you know these things, you will be blessed if you do them.

"I'm not speaking of all of you. I know the ones I chose. But this is to fulfill the Scripture, 'The one who eats bread with me has lifted up his heel against me.' I'm telling you this before it happens so when it happens you may believe that I am he.

"I tell you the truth, the one who welcomes whomever I send welcomes me. And the one who welcomes me welcomes the one who sent me."

After Jesus had said these things and while they were still reclining at the table and eating, he became deeply troubled and said, "I'm telling you the truth: One of you will betray me, even someone who is eating with me!"

The disciples became extremely distressed and looked around at each other, wondering who he meant. They began to ask each other which one of them might do this. One by one they asked him, "Lord, am I the one?"

He said to them, "It is one of the twelve, one who is dipping his hand in the dish with me. Look, the hand of the one who is betraying me is with me on the table. The Son of Man will indeed go as it has been determined and predicted in the Scriptures. But how awful it will be for the one who betrays him! It would have been better for that man if he had never been born."

Then Judas asked him, "Rabbi, am I the one?"

"You have said it yourself," Jesus replied.

One of his disciples—the one Jesus loved—was reclining next to him. So Simon Peter motioned to this disciple to find out from Jesus who he meant. The disciple leaned closer to Jesus and said, "Lord, who is it?"

Jesus answered, "It's the one I give this piece of bread to after I have dipped it in the dish." After dipping the piece of bread, he gave it to Judas Iscariot, son of Simon. Judas took it, and immediately Satan entered into him.

Then Jesus said to him, "What you're doing, do quickly." None of those at the table knew why Jesus said this to him. Some thought that since Judas had charge of the money bag, Jesus was telling him to buy what they needed for the feast or that he should give something to the poor.

Immediately after Judas took the piece of bread, he left. And it was night.

After he had gone, Jesus said, "Now the Son of Man has been glorified, and God has been glorified in him. If God has been glorified in him, God will also glorify him in himself—and he will glorify him very soon.

"Little children, I am with you for only a little while longer. You will look for me, but just as I said to the Jews, 'You cannot come where I am going,' so I now say it also to you."

As they were eating, Jesus took the bread and blessed it. When he had given thanks, he broke it and gave it to the disciples. "Take it and eat it," he told them. "This is my body, which is given for you. Do this to remember me."

In the same way after the supper he took a cup. When he had given thanks, he gave it to them and said, "Drink from it, all of you." And they all drank from it.

He told them, "This cup which is poured out for you is my blood of the new covenant, which is poured out on behalf of many people for the forgiveness of sins. I tell you the truth, I will not drink again from this fruit of the vine until the day I drink it fresh with you in the kingdom of my Father."

The Last Supper

An argument arose among them about who was considered the greatest. So Jesus said to them, "The kings of the nations lord it over their subjects, and those in authority are called benefactors. But it isn't to be that way among you. The greatest among you must become like the youngest, and your leader must become a servant. For who is greater: the one who reclines at the table to eat, or the one who serves? Is it not the one at the table? Yet I am among you as the one who serves.

"I am giving you a new commandment: you must love each other. Love each other just as I have loved you. Everyone will know you are my disciples if you love each other."

Peter said to him, "Lord, where are you going?"

"Where I am going you cannot follow now," Jesus answered. "But afterward you will. You disciples have stayed with me through my trials, and just as my Father granted a kingdom to me, so I am granting one to you: that you may eat and drink at my table in my kingdom and sit on thrones to judge the twelve tribes of Israel."

"Lord, why can't I follow you now?" Peter said. "I'll give up my life for you."

"Will you give up your life for me?" Jesus answered. "Simon, Simon, listen! Satan has demanded to have you disciples that he might sift you like wheat. But

I have prayed for you, Peter that your faith will not fail. And when you have come back, strengthen your brothers."

"Lord," said Peter, "I'm ready to go with you even to prison and death!"

But Jesus replied, "I'm telling you the truth, Peter: The rooster will not crow at all today until you have denied three times that you know me!

"Don't let your hearts be troubled. You believe in God; believe in me as well. In my Father's house are many permanent residences. If it were not so, I would have told you. I go to prepare a place for you. And if I go to prepare a place for you, I will come again and take you to be with me that you may be where I am. You know where I am going, and you know the way."

"Lord, we don't know where you're going," Thomas said. "How can we know the way?"

Jesus answered, "I am the way and the truth and the life. No one comes to the Father except through me. If you had known me, you also would have known my Father. From now on you know him and have seen him."

"Lord, show us the Father," Philip said, "and we will be satisfied."

Jesus replied, "Have I been so long with you all, Philip, and yet you don't know me? Whoever has seen me has seen the Father. How can you say, 'Show us the Father'? Do you not believe I am in the Father and that the Father is in me? What I say to you I'm not saying on my own, but the Father who lives in me is doing his work. Believe me that I am in the Father and the Father is in me—or at least believe me because of the miracles themselves.

"I'm telling you the truth: whoever believes in me will do the same kind of things I am doing. He will do even greater works than these because I am going to my Father. I will do whatever you ask in my name, so the Father will be glorified in the Son. If you ask anything in my name, I will do it.

"If you love me, keep my commandments. And I will ask the Father, and he will give you another Helper— the Spirit of truth, to live with you forever. The world cannot receive him because it neither sees him nor knows him. But you know him because he is living with you and will be in you.

"I will not leave you as orphans; I will come to you. In a little while the world will see me no longer, but you will see me. Because I live, you will also live. At that time you will know I am in my Father, and you are in me, and I am in you.

"The one who has my commandments and keeps them is the one who loves me. And the one who loves me will be loved by my Father, and I will love him and will disclose myself to him."

Judas (not Iscariot) said to him, "Lord, how is it that you will disclose yourself to us but not to the world?"

"If anyone loves me," Jesus answered, "he will keep my word. And my Father will love him, and we will come to him and live with him. The one who doesn't love me does not keep my words. The word you are hearing is not my own but comes from the Father who sent me.

"I have told you these things while I am with you. But the Helper, the Holy Spirit whom the Father will send in my name, will teach you everything and help you remember everything I told you.

"Peace I leave with you. My peace I am giving you. I do not give to you as the world does. Don't let your hearts be troubled and don't let them be afraid.

"You heard me say, 'I'm going away,' and 'I'm coming to you.' If you loved me, you would have been very happy to hear me say, 'I am going to the Father,' because my Father is greater than I am. I've told you this before it happens so that when it happens you may believe.

"I won't speak with you any longer, because the ruler of this world is coming. But he has no claim on me, and I do just what the Father commanded me so the world will know I love the Father. Get up, let's leave.

"I am the true vine, and my Father is the keeper of the vineyard. He takes up every branch in me that doesn't bear fruit. And he cleanses every branch that does bear fruit so it may bear more fruit. You are already clean through the word I have spoken to you.

"Abide in me, and I will abide in you. Just as the branch cannot bear fruit by itself unless it abides in the vine, so neither can you unless you abide in me. I am the vine, you are the branches; the one who abides in me, and I in him, will bear much fruit. Apart from me you can do nothing.

"If anyone does not abide in me, he is thrown out as a branch and withers. Then they gather the branches and throw them into the fire, and they burn up.

"If you abide in me and my words abide in you, you may ask whatever you want and it will be done for you. My Father is glorified when you bear much fruit. This way you will mature as my disciples.

"As the Father has loved me, so have I loved you. Continue in my love. If you keep my commandments, you will continue in my love, just as I have kept my Father's commandments and have continued in his love.

"I've said these things to you so my joy may continue in you and that your joy may be full.

"This is my commandment: love each other just as I have loved you. No one has any greater love than the one who gives up his life for his friends.

"You are my friends if you do everything I command you. I don't call you servants any longer because the servant doesn't know what his master is doing. But I have called you friends because everything I heard from my Father I have made known to you. You did not choose me, but I chose you and appointed you to go and bear fruit—and that your fruit will remain. Then the Father will give you whatever you ask in my name.

"I am giving you these commands so you may love each other.

"If the world hates you, you know that it hated me before you. If you belonged to the world, the world would love its own. But because you do not belong to the world—instead, I chose you out of the world— the world hates you. Remember what I said to you: 'A servant isn't greater than his master.' If they persecuted me, they will also persecute you. If they kept my word, they will also keep yours. But they will do all these things to you on account of me because they don't know the one who sent me.

"If I had not come and spoken to them, they wouldn't be guilty of sin. But now they have no excuse for their sin. The one who hates me also hates my Father. If I had not performed miracles among them as no one else performed, they wouldn't have become guilty of sin. But now they have both seen and hated me and my Father. In that way, what was written in their law has been fulfilled: 'They hated me without a reason.'

"When the Helper has come whom I will send from the Father—the Spirit of truth who comes from the Father—he will testify about me. You, too, are giving testimony because you have been with me from the beginning.

"I have said these things to you so you will not stumble. They will banish you from the synagogues. In fact, the time is coming when whoever kills you will think he is serving God. They will do these things to you because they know neither the Father nor me. But I have said these things to you so that, whenever the time comes, you will remember that I told you.

"I did not tell you these things at first because I was with you, but now I'm going away to the one who sent me. And none of you is asking, 'Where are you going?' Instead, because I have said these things to you, you are filled with sorrow. Even so, I'm telling you the truth: it's profitable for you that I leave. If I don't go, the Helper will not come to you. But if I go, I will send him to you.

"When he has come, he will convict the world of sin and righteousness and judgment. Of sin because they don't believe in me, of righteousness, because I am going away to the Father and you won't see me anymore, and of judgment because the ruler of this world has been judged.

"I still have many things to say to you, but you cannot bear them now. But when he, the Spirit of truth, has come, he will guide you into all the truth. He will not speak on his own authority, but he will speak whatever he hears. He will tell you about things yet to come. He will glorify me because he will take from what is mine and will tell it to you. Everything the Father has is mine. That is why I said he will take from what is mine and show it to you.

"In a little while you won't see me, and again in a little while you will see me."

Some of the disciples said to each other, "What does he mean, 'In a little while you won't see me, and again in a little while you will see me,' and, 'Because I am going away to the Father'? What does he mean, 'in a little while'? We don't understand what he's saying."

Jesus knew they wanted to question him. He said to them, "Are you asking each other what I meant when I said, 'In a little while you won't see me, and again in a little while you will see me'? I tell you the truth, you will weep and mourn, but the world will be glad. You will grieve, but your sorrow will turn into joy. When a woman is giving birth, she is in pain because her time has come. But after she has given birth to the child, she forgets the pain because of the joy that a child has been born into the world. In the same way, you are now saddened, but I will see you again, and you will be glad. No one will take away your joy. When that day comes, you will ask me nothing.

"I tell you the truth, the Father will give you whatever you may request from him in my name. As yet you have asked for nothing in my name. Ask, and you will receive so your joy will be made complete.

"I have spoken to you about these things in veiled figures. But the time is coming when I will speak no longer in figures but will tell you plainly about the Father. When that day comes, you will ask in my name.

"I'm not saying I will make petitions to the Father on your behalf, because the Father himself loves you, since you have loved me and have believed that I came from God.

"I came from the Father and have come into the world. Now I am leaving the world and returning to the Father."

His disciples said to him, "Now you're speaking plainly and not in figures of speech. Now we know that you know everything and don't need anyone to question you. Because of this we believe you really did come from God."

Jesus answered them, "Now do you believe? Understand this: the time is coming—and has already arrived—when you will be scattered, each of you to his own home, and you will leave me all alone. Yet I am not alone because the Father is with me. I have told you these things so that in me you might have peace. In the world you have trouble, but take heart! I have overcome the world."

Jesus looked up to heaven after he had said these things, and he said, "Father, the time has come. Glorify your Son so your Son may glorify you—just as you gave him authority over all mankind so he might give eternal life to everyone you gave to him. And this is eternal life: that they might know you, the only true God, and Jesus Christ, whom you sent.

"I glorified you on earth. I finished the work you gave me to do. Now, Father, glorify me together with yourself, with the glory I had with you before the world existed.

"I made your name known to the men you have given to me out of the world. They were yours; you have given them to me, and they have kept your word. Now they know that everything comes from you, all the things you have given me. I have given them the words you gave to me. They accepted them and were convinced that I came from you. They believed you sent me.

"I am praying for them. I don't pray for the world but for those you have given me because they belong to you. Everyone who belongs to me also belongs to you. All who belong to you belong to me, and I have been glorified in them. Now I am no longer in the world, but these are in the world, and I am coming to you. Holy Father, keep those whom you have given to me in your name so they may be one, even as we are one.

"While I was in the world, I kept them in your name. I guarded those you gave me, and none of them has been lost except the son of perdition, in order to fulfill the Scripture. But now I am coming to you. I am speaking these things while still in the world so they may experience my joy to the fullest degree.

"I have given them your word, and the world has begun to hate them because they don't belong to the world any more than I belong to the world. I don't pray that you would take them out of the world but that you would keep them from the evil one. They do not belong to the world any more than I belong to the world. Set them apart and make them holy in your truth; your word is truth. As you sent me into the world, even so I am sending them into the world. For their sakes I set myself apart and make myself holy, so that they also may be set apart and made holy in truth.

"I don't pray for these men only but also for those who will believe in me through their testimony. I pray that they will all be one just as you, Father, are in me, and I am in you. I pray that they may be one in us so the world may believe you sent me.

"I have given them the glory that you gave me so they may be one even as we are one—I in them and you in me. I pray that they may be perfectly one and that the world may know that you sent me and have loved them just as you loved me.

"Father, I desire that those you have given me may be with me where I am. Permit them to see my glory, which you gave me in love before the world was founded. Righteous Father, the world did not know you, but I knew you, and these men knew you sent me. I made your name known to them, and I will make it known again, so your love for me may be in them and I in them."

Then Jesus said to them, "Did you lack anything when I sent you out without a purse or bag or sandals?"

And they replied, "No, nothing."

"But now," he said, "take a purse if you have it. The same goes for a bag. And if you don't have a sword, go sell your cloak and buy one. I'm telling you that this

Scripture must yet be fulfilled in my life: 'And he was counted among the sinners.' The things concerning me have their fulfillment."

"Look, Lord," they said, "here are two swords."

He replied, "It is enough."

After they had sung a hymn, Jesus left for the Mount of Olives (as was his custom), and his disciples followed him.

Then Jesus said to them, "All of you will fall away on my account tonight, for it is written, 'I will strike the shepherd, and the sheep of the flock will be scattered.' But after being raised up I will go ahead of you into Galilee."

"Even if everyone else falls away on your account," Peter stated, "I won't. I will never fall away."

"I tell you the truth," Jesus told him, "this very night, before the rooster crows twice, you will deny me three times."

Peter responded even more vehemently. "Even if I must die with you, I'll never deny you!"

And all the disciples said the same thing.

CRUCIFIXION, RESURRECTION, AND ASCENSION

Passover AD 33

Then Jesus went with his disciples across the Kidron Valley to a garden called Gethsemane. When they had entered the place, he said to them, "Sit here while I go over there and pray."

He took with him Peter and the two sons of Zebedee, James and John, and began to be deeply grieved with great distress and agony. Then he said to them, "My soul is extremely sorrowful even to the point of death. Stay here and watch with me. Pray that you may not be tempted."

Then he went a little farther away, about the distance of a stone's throw, knelt on the ground, and fell on his face. He prayed that, if it were possible, this time

The Agony in the Garden

of agony might pass from him. "Abba, Father," he said, "everything is possible for you. My Father, if it is possible, let this cup pass from me. Yet do not do what I will but what you will."

He returned to the disciples and found them sleeping. He said to Peter, "Simon, are you asleep? So you couldn't watch with me for even one hour! Watch and pray that you may not be tempted. The spirit is willing, but the flesh is weak."

A second time he went off and prayed. "My Father," he said, "if you are willing, take away this cup from me. Yet if this cannot pass from me unless I drink it, do your will and not my own."

Then an angel from heaven appeared to him and strengthened him. He was in agony and prayed even more fervently, and his sweat became like large drops of blood falling to the ground.

When he got up from praying, he returned to the disciples and found them sleeping again, exhausted from sorrow, for their eyes were heavy. He said to them, "Why are you sleeping? Get up and pray so you may not be tempted!"

They didn't know how to respond. So he left them and went off again and prayed a third time, saying the same things as before.

Then for the third time he returned to the disciples and said to them, "Are you still sleeping and getting some rest? It's enough! See, the hour has come and the Son of Man is being betrayed into the hands of sinners. Get up and let's go. Look, my betrayer is approaching!"

A large crowd approached while he was still speaking. The man named Judas, one of the twelve, was leading them. Judas also knew the place because Jesus had often gone there with his disciples. So Judas came there, accompanied by a cohort of soldiers, officers from the chief priests, Pharisees, teachers of the law, and the elders of the people, all bearing torches and lanterns and swords and clubs.

The betrayer had given them a signal. He told them, "It's the one I kiss. Seize him and lead him safely away."

As soon as he arrived, he approached Jesus to kiss him. "My friend," Jesus said to him, "why have you come?"

"Greetings, Master!" Judas said. And he kissed him.

"Judas," Jesus said, "do you betray the Son of Man with a kiss?"

Jesus knew everything that was about to happen to him. He stepped forward and said to them, "Who do you want?"

"Jesus of Nazareth!" they answered.

Jesus replied, "I am."

Judas, the man betraying him, was standing with them. When Jesus said, "I am," they all drew back and fell to the ground.

Again he asked, "Who do you want?"

"Jesus of Nazareth," they said.

"I told you I am," Jesus said. "If you're after me, then let these others go away." (He said this so the words he spoke might be fulfilled: "I lost none of those you gave me.")

Then they came and gruffly seized Jesus. When those who were standing around saw what was about to happen, they said to him, "Lord, should we strike them with the sword?"

Simon Peter drew his sword and struck the high priest's servant, cutting off his right ear. (The servant's name was Malchus.)

But Jesus said, "Enough of this!" he touched the man's ear and healed him.

Then he told Peter, "Put your sword back into its sheath. Everyone who uses the sword will die by the sword. Don't you understand that even now I could call to my Father and he would send me more than twelve legions of angels? But then how would the Scriptures be fulfilled that say it must happen like this? Shall I not drink the cup the Father has given me?"

At that same time Jesus said to the crowds and to the chief priests, the captains of the temple, and the elders, who had come out to arrest him, "Have you come out to seize me with swords and clubs as if I were a robber? I sat daily with you, teaching in the temple, yet you didn't arrest me or stretch out your hands against me. But this has all happened to fulfill the Scriptures of the prophets. This is your hour and the power of darkness."

Then all the disciples abandoned him and ran away. A young man was following him, clothed only in a linen cloth, and some other young men grabbed him. But he ran away from them naked, leaving behind the linen cloth.

Then the cohort of soldiers and the chief captain and the officers of the Jews took and bound Jesus.

They led him away first to Annas because he was the father-in-law of Caiaphas, who was the high priest that year. (It was Caiaphas who had advised the Jews that it would be prudent for one man to die for the people.)

The high priest questioned Jesus about his disciples and his teaching. Jesus answered him, "I spoke openly to the world. I always taught in the synagogues and in the temple where all the Jews assemble. I said nothing in secret. Why do you question me? Question those who heard me. They know what I said."

When he said this, one of the officers standing nearby struck Jesus in the face. "Is this the way you answer the high priest?" he demanded.

"If I spoke wrongly," Jesus answered, "explain my error. But if I have spoken rightly, why do you strike me?"

Then Annas sent him, still bound, to Caiaphas the high priest. Those who had seized Jesus led him away to the high priest's house, where all the chief priests and the elders and teachers of the law had gathered.

Simon Peter and another disciple kept following Jesus from a distance, even up to the courtyard of the high priest. The other disciple was known to the high priest and went into the courtyard with Jesus, but Peter stood outside the door. Then the other disciple went out and spoke to the servant girl who tended the door and brought Peter in.

The servant girl then said to Peter, "Aren't you one of this man's disciples?"

"I am not," Peter replied.

Because it was cold, the servants and temple guards had started a fire of coals in the middle of the courtyard and were standing by it, warming themselves. Peter was standing with them by the fire, warming himself. When they had all sat down, he sat down as well in the middle of the guards to see what would happen.

"Aren't you also one of his disciples?" they asked him. Peter denied it. "I am not!" he said.

The chief priests and the elders and the entire Sanhedrin kept trying to find false witnesses to testify against Jesus in order to execute him. They could find none. Though many false witnesses came forward to accuse him, their testimony did not agree.

At last two stepped forward and spoke against him: "We heard this man say, 'I'll destroy this temple of God made by human hands, and in three days I'll build another, not made by human hands.'" But even then their statements did not agree.

So the high priest stood up before them and questioned Jesus. "Do you refuse to answer?" he demanded. "What is this they're accusing you of?"

But Jesus was silent and made no answer.

Once more the high priest said to him, "Are you the Messiah, the Son of the Blessed One? I charge you under oath by the living God: tell us whether you're the Messiah, the Son of God."

"It's just as you have said," Jesus answered. "I am. Furthermore, I tell all of you that later on you will see the Son of Man sitting by the right hand of power and coming on the clouds of heaven."

Then the high priest tore his clothes and said, "He has spoken blasphemy! Why do we need any

St. Peter Denying Christ

more witnesses? Listen, you have heard his blasphemy. What do you think?"

"He deserves to die!" they answered. Everyone condemned him as deserving death.

Some of them began to spit in his face and strike him with their fists. The men who were holding Jesus began to mock him. After they had blindfolded him, they kept slapping his face and taunting him. "Prophesy!" they said. "Prophesy to us, you 'Messiah'! Who just struck you?"

And they said many other insulting things to him.

Meanwhile Simon Peter was sitting below, out in the courtyard. One of the high priest's servant girls saw Peter warming himself. She looked intently at him where he sat in the light and said, "This man, too, was with Jesus of Nazareth."

She went closer to him and said, "You, too, were with the Galilean."

But Peter denied it in front of them all. "Woman, I don't know him!" he said. "I don't even know what you're talking about." Then he went out to the courtyard's entryway [and a rooster crowed.]

A little later, when he had gone out to the gate, another woman saw him and said to those nearby, "This man, too, was with Jesus the Nazarene."

Another man saw him and said, "You, too, are one of them!"

But Peter again denied it, this time with an oath: "I don't know the Man!"

The servant girl saw him again. "This man is one of them," she began saying to those nearby. Again Peter denied it.

About an hour later another man spoke up and insisted, "Without a doubt this man was with him because he too is a Galilean."

Then one of the servants of the high priest (a relative of the man whose ear Peter had cut off) said, "Didn't I see you in the garden with him?" The others standing there came close to Peter and said, "Certainly you're also one of them! You're a Galilean—your speech betrays you!"

But Peter denied it again and began to curse and swear. "I don't know this fellow you're talking about," he shouted. "I don't know what you're saying!"

While he was still speaking, a rooster crowed a second time, and the Lord turned and looked at Peter. Then Peter remembered what the Lord had told him: "Before the rooster crows, you will deny me three times," and, "Before it crows the second time, you will deny me three times."

Peter went out and wept uncontrollably, with bitter tears.

As soon as daylight came, all the elders of the people—both the chief priests and the teachers of the law—met together against Jesus to execute him. They brought him up to the whole Sanhedrin and said, "If you are the Messiah, tell us."

He said to them, "If I were to tell you, you would certainly not believe. And if I were to ask the questions, you would not answer me or let me go. But from now on the Son of Man will be seated by the right hand of the power of God!"

"So you are the Son of God?" they all said.

"It's just as you say," he replied, "because I am."

"Why do we need further witnesses?" they said. "We have heard it ourselves from his own mouth!"

Then the whole crowd arose and tied up Jesus and took him to appear before Pontius Pilate, the governor.

When Judas, who had betrayed him, saw that Jesus was condemned, he was overcome with remorse. He returned the thirty pieces of silver to the chief priests and the elders and said to them, "I have sinned by betraying the blood of an innocent man!"

"What does that matter to us?" they replied. "Deal with that yourself."

Judas threw down the pieces of silver in the temple, left, and went out and hung himself.

The chief priests took the silver pieces and said, "It isn't legal to put these in the treasury since this is blood money."

(After discussing the matter they used the money to buy the potter's field as a burying ground for foreigners. That is why even today it is called the Field of Blood. In this way the words of Jeremiah the prophet were fulfilled: "And they took the thirty pieces of silver, the price at which he was valued by the sons of Israel, and used them to buy the potter's field, as the Lord directed me.")

Then the Jews led Jesus from Caiaphas to the Roman judgment hall, where Jesus stood before the governor. Because it was early, they did not go into the judgment hall. (They didn't want to become defiled and be unable to eat the Passover.)

So Pilate went out to them. "Of what are you accusing this man?" he asked them.

"If he were not a criminal," they answered, "we wouldn't have brought him to you."

"Take him and judge him according to your law," Pilate replied.

"We aren't permitted to execute anyone," the Jews responded. (In this way they were fulfilling what Jesus said about the kind of death he would suffer.) They began accusing him, saying, "We found this man subverting our nation and forbidding us to give tribute to Caesar. He says he's the Messiah, a king."

The chief priests and elders continued making many accusations against Jesus. But he made no reply.

"Do you refuse to answer?" Pilate said. "Don't you hear how many accusations they're charging you with?"

Jesus remained silent, not answering a single charge. The governor was astonished.

Pilate then went back to the judgment hall and called Jesus. "Are you the king of the Jews?" he asked him.

Jesus replied, "It's just as you say. Are you asking this on your own, or did others tell you about me?"

"Am I a Jew?" Pilate answered. "Your own nation and the chief priests handed you over to me. What have you done?"

Jesus said, "My kingdom is not of this world. If my kingdom were of this world, my servants would fight to keep me from being handed over to the Jews. But at present my kingdom is not from here."

"Then you really are a king?" Pilate said.

Jesus answered, "It's just as you say. I am a king—I was born for this, and for this I came into the world, so I might testify to the truth. Everyone who belongs to the truth hears my voice."

"What is truth?" Pilate asked.

After saying this, Pilate went out again to the Jews and said to the chief priests and the crowds, "I find this man guilty of nothing."

But they strongly insisted, "He is stirring up the people. He is teaching throughout Judea, starting from Galilee and reaching even to this place."

When Pilate heard this, he asked whether the man was a Galilean. On learning that he was from the jurisdiction of Herod, he sent him up to Herod, who happened to be in Jerusalem at the time.

When Herod saw Jesus, he was quite pleased. For a long time he had wanted to see him since he had heard many reports about him and hoped to see him perform some miracle. He probed him with many questions. But Jesus didn't answer them even though the priests and teachers of the law stood there viciously accusing him.

After Herod and his soldiers had ridiculed and mocked him, they clothed him in a gaudy robe and sent him back to Pilate. From that day on Pilate and Herod became friends; before this they did not get along.

Then Pilate called together the chief priests and the rulers of the people and said to them, "You brought this man to me on the charge of stirring up subversion. Yet on examining him I found no substance to your accusations. Neither did Herod because he sent him back to us. You can see he's done nothing deserving death.

"Now, you have a custom directing me to release one man to you at Passover. So I'll punish him and then release him." (At the feast the governor's custom was to release one prisoner to the people, whomever they chose. At that time a notable prisoner named Barabbas was being held along with a few of his fellow insurgents. He was a robber who had been thrown into prison for an insurrection in the city and for murder.)

When the crowds had gathered and noisily asked Pilate to act on the custom, he answered, "Whom do you want me to release to you? Barabbas, or Jesus, who is called 'Messiah'?" (He knew the chief priests had handed Jesus over because of envy. And as he was sitting on the judgment seat, his wife sent word to him: "Don't do anything to that just man! On account of him I have suffered many things today in a dream!")

But the chief priests and the elders stirred up the crowds to ask Pilate to release Barabbas to them instead, and to execute Jesus.

"Which of the two do you want me to release to you?" the governor said. "Do you want me to release to you the king of the Jews?"

They replied, "Barabbas!" They all shouted together, "Not this man! Get rid of him, and give us Barabbas!"

Because Pilate wanted to release Jesus, he said to them once more, "Then what should I do with Jesus who is called 'Messiah,' whom you call 'King of the Jews'?"

Again they all shouted, "Let him be crucified!" They continued crying out, "Crucify! Crucify him!"

For the third time Pilate said to them, "Why, what evil has he done? I don't find that he's done anything deserving death. So after punishing him, I'll release him."

Pilate took Jesus and had him flogged. The soldiers took thorns, wove them into a crown, and placed it on his head. They put a purple garment on him and said, "Hail, King of the Jews!" and kept punching him with their fists.

Pilate then came out again and said to them, "Look, I am bringing him out to you so you'll know I find him not guilty." Jesus came out, wearing the crown of thorns and the purple garment. "Look at the man!" Pilate said to them.

When the chief priests and the officers saw him, they shouted, "Crucify! Crucify!"

"You take him and crucify him yourself," Pilate said. "I find him not guilty."

Christ Mocked

"We have a law," the Jews answered, "and by our law he ought to die because he claimed to be the Son of God."

When Pilate heard this claim, he grew even more afraid. He returned to the judgment hall and said to Jesus, "Where do you come from?"

Jesus gave no answer.

"You refuse to talk to me?" Pilate said. "Don't you know I have authority to crucify you—or to release you?"

Jesus answered, "You would have no authority at all over me unless it had been given to you from above. Because of this the one who handed me over to you is guilty of the greater sin."

These words prompted Pilate to continue seeking ways to release him. But the Jews shouted, "If you release this man, you're no friend of Caesar. Anyone claiming to be the king is speaking against Caesar!"

Hearing this, Pilate brought Jesus outside. He sat down on the judgment seat in a place called the Pavement (or in the Jewish language, "Gabbatha"). It was Preparation Day for the Passover, about six in the morning. He said to the Jews, "Look at your king."

But they shouted, "Away with him! Away with him! Crucify him!" They were insistent and shouted all the more, demanding loudly that he be crucified.

Pilate said to them, "Should I crucify your king?"

"We have no king," the chief priests answered, "except Caesar!"

When Pilate saw he couldn't dissuade them, but instead a riot was in the making, he took water and washed his hands in front of the crowd and said, "I am innocent of the blood of this righteous man. You will be witnesses of the fact."

All the people answered, "His blood be on us and on our children!"

Their voices and those of the chief priests won out. So Pilate, wanting to satisfy the crowd, ordered that they should get what they demanded. He released Barabbas to them—the man they had asked for, who had been thrown into prison for insurrection and murder—but he gave in to their demands about Jesus and handed him over to be crucified.

Then the governor's soldiers took Jesus and led him away to the court called the Praetorium. There they gathered the whole company of soldiers around him. They stripped him, then again clothed him in purple, and put a crimson cloak on him. And they put on his head the crown of thorns they had made, and placed a reed in his right hand. They continued mocking him, bowing in homage and saying "Hail, 'King' of the Jews!" They spat on him and took the reed from him and kept beating him on his head.

When they finished ridiculing him, the soldiers stripped him of the cloak and the purple garments and gave him his own clothing. Then they led him out to crucify him.

Jesus went out, carrying his own cross. As they were going, they found a passerby from Cyrene coming in from the country. He was named Simon, the father of Alexander and Rufus. They grabbed him, laid the cross on him, and forced him to carry it behind Jesus.

A large crowd followed him, including women who were weeping and mourning for him. But Jesus turned to them and said, "Daughters of Jerusalem, don't weep for me but for yourselves and for your children. The days are coming when they will say, 'Blessed are the childless, and the wombs that never bore children, and the breasts that never nursed!' Then they will begin to say to the mountains, 'Fall on us!' and to the hills, 'Cover us!' For if they do these things when the tree is green, what will happen when it is dry?"

Two others, who were criminals, were led away with him to be executed.

When they brought him to the place called the Skull (or in the Jewish language, "Golgotha," ["Calvary" in Latin]), they offered him wine mixed with myrrh, but when he tasted it, he wouldn't drink.

There, at nine o'clock, they crucified him.

"Father, forgive them," Jesus said, "because they do not know what they are doing."

Along with him they crucified the criminals, two robbers, one on either side and Jesus in the middle.

[And the Scripture was fulfilled which says, "And he was numbered with transgressors."]

Pilate also wrote an inscription, which they placed on the cross above his head. The accusation said,

THIS IS
JESUS OF NAZARETH
THE KING OF THE JEWS

Many Jews read this inscription (it was written in the Jewish language, in Latin, and in Greek), since the place where Jesus was crucified was near the city. So the chief priests of the Jews said to Pilate, "Don't write, 'The King of the Jews,' but rather, 'he said, "I am King of the Jews."'"

Pilate answered, "What I have written, I have written."

When the soldiers had crucified Jesus, they took his clothes and divided them into four equal parts, and rolled dice to see who would get each part. They left out the undergarment, however, which was of one piece, woven from the top down. "Let's not tear it," they said, "but roll for it, to see who will get it." So the Scripture was fulfilled that says, "They divided my garments among themselves, and for my clothing they rolled the dice."

This, therefore, is what the soldiers did. Then they sat down to keep guard over him.

Meanwhile the people stood watching. Those who passed by kept jeering him, wagging their heads and saying, "Aha! You who would 'destroy the temple and build it in three days,' save yourself! If you're the Son of God, come down from the cross!"

In the same way the chief priests, the teachers of the law, and the elders mocked him.

"He 'saved' others," they said, "yet he can't save himself."

"Let him save himself, if he's the Christ, the chosen one of God!"

"If he's the king of Israel, let the Messiah come down now from the cross so we may see and believe!"

"He trusted in God; let God deliver him now if he wants him—since he said, 'I'm the Son of God.'"

The soldiers also kept mocking him. They came to him offering sour wine and said to him, "If you're the king of the Jews, save yourself."

The robbers who had been crucified with him started to reproach him in the same manner. One of the criminals continued to bitterly scorn him.

"Aren't you the Messiah?" he said. "Then save your-self and us!"

But the other rebuked him and said, "Don't you even fear God since you're under the same punish-ment this man is? We've been punished justly—we're receiving only what our actions deserve. But this man did nothing wrong!"

"Jesus," he said, "remember me when you come into your kingdom."

"I tell you the truth," Jesus answered, "today you will be with me in Paradise."

It was about noon. Standing by the cross of Jesus were his mother and his mother's sister, as well as Mary the wife of Clopas and Mary Magdalene. When Jesus saw his mother and the disciple whom he loved standing nearby, he said to his mother, "Woman, here is your son."

Then he said to the disciple, "Here is your mother."

From that moment on, this disciple took her into his home.

From noon until three in the afternoon, darkness covered the whole land and the sun was obscured. At three o'clock Jesus said in a loud voice, "Eloi, Eloi, lama sabachthani?" (which means, "My God, my God, why have you forsaken me?").

The Crucifixion

When some of those who were standing there heard it, they said, "Look, this man is calling for Elijah."

And now Jesus, knowing that everything was accomplished, said the words "I am thirsty" in fulfillment of Scripture. A jar of sour wine was sitting there, and one of the men ran to it at once. He took a sponge, filled it with the wine, put it on a hyssop stalk, and lifted it to Jesus' mouth. "Let him drink," he and the others said. "Let's see if Elijah comes to take him down and save him."

After taking the wine, Jesus again cried out in a loud voice, "It is finished!"

Then he bowed his head. "Father," he said, "into your hands I commit my spirit."

After saying these words, he yielded up his spirit and breathed his last.

When the centurion standing nearby heard Jesus cry out and saw how he died, he gave glory to God and said, "Truly, this was a righteous man!"

At that moment the veil of the temple was torn in two from top to bottom. The earth shook, the rocks broke in pieces, and the tombs were opened, and many bodies of the saints who had died rose again. They came out of the tombs after Jesus' resurrection, entered the holy city and appeared to many people.

The centurion and those with him who were standing guard over Jesus were struck with fear when they saw the earthquake and the things that took place. They said, "Surely this man was God's Son!" The crowds who had come to see the crucifixion also saw these things and returned home, beating their breasts.

Those who knew Jesus and the women who had followed him from Galilee all stood at a distance and saw these things. Among them were Mary Magdalene, Mary the mother of James the younger and of Joses, and Salome the mother of the sons of Zebedee—women who had followed him and ministered to him in Galilee (along with many others who came up with him to Jerusalem).

Since it was Preparation Day (for that Sabbath was a special day), the Jews, in order to keep the bodies from remaining on the cross on the Sabbath, asked Pilate to have their legs broken and then have them taken away. So the soldiers came and broke the legs of the two men who were crucified with Jesus. But when they came to Jesus and saw that he had already died, they did not break his legs. Instead, one of the soldiers pierced his side with a spear, and immediately blood and water came out.

The one who saw this has given this testimony (his testimony is true, and he knows he tells the truth) so you may believe. These things happened so the Scripture might be fulfilled: "Not one of his bones will be broken." And another Scripture says, "They will look on the one they pierced."

After this, when it was already evening, a man named Joseph went to Pilate. He was a rich man from the Jewish city of Arimathea and a disciple of Jesus (though he kept it secret because he was afraid of the Jews). He was a reputable member of the Sanhedrin, a good and just man who had not agreed with its decision and actions. He was also looking for the kingdom of God. Since it was the Preparation, the day before the Sabbath, he boldly went to Pilate and asked for permission to take away the body of Jesus.

Pilate was surprised to hear that he was dead so soon, so he called for the centurion and asked whether Jesus had already died. On learning it was so, he granted the body to Joseph.

Joseph then bought fine linen cloth and went and took down the body. Nicodemus also came—the man who at the beginning came to Jesus at night—bringing a mixture of myrrh and aloes weighing about seventy-five pounds. They took away the body of Jesus and wrapped it in the clean linen cloths along with the spices, according to the Jewish burial custom.

Near the place where he was crucified was a garden, and in it was an unused tomb that Joseph had newly carved out of the rock. Since this was the Preparation Day and the Sabbath was imminent, they laid Jesus there because the tomb was so close. Then they rolled a large stone against the door of the tomb and left.

The women who came with Jesus from Galilee had followed—Mary Magdalene and the other Mary, the mother of Joses—and as they sat across from the tomb, they saw where and how his body was laid. Then they returned home and prepared spices and ointments. They rested on the Sabbath day in observance of the commandment.

The morning after the Preparation Day the chief priests and the Pharisees gathered before Pilate and said, "Sir, we remember that while he was still alive the impostor said, 'After three days I will rise again.' So give the order to secure the grave until the third day, or else his disciples will come at night and steal his body and say to the people, 'He has risen from the dead.' Then the last deception will be worse than the first."

Pilate told them, "You have a guard; go and make the tomb as secure as you can." So they went and made the tomb secure, sealing the stone and stationing the guard.

When the Sabbath was over, Mary Magdalene and the other Mary (the mother of James) and Salome bought spices which they intended to use to anoint Jesus' body. They and several others with them came at early dawn on the first day of the week to see the tomb, bringing along the spices they had prepared.

Suddenly there was a powerful earthquake. An angel of the Lord descended from heaven, came and rolled the stone away from the door, and sat on it. He shone like lightning, and his clothes were as white as snow. The guards were terrified and became like dead men.

[Now after Jesus rose, early on the first day of the week, he appeared first to Mary Magdalene, out of whom he had cast seven demons.] Mary came to the tomb while it was still dark and saw that the stone had been rolled away from the door. Then she ran to Simon Peter and to the other disciple, the one Jesus loved, and said to them, "They took away the Lord from the tomb! And we don't know where they laid him."

Then Peter and the other disciple went out and ran toward the tomb. They started out running together, but the other disciple outran Peter and reached the tomb first. He stooped down and saw the linen cloths lying there but didn't go in. Simon Peter arrived shortly afterward and went into the tomb. [Stooping down,] he saw the linen cloths lying [by themselves]. The face cloth which had been around his head was lying not with the linen cloths but folded up in a place by itself.

Then the disciple who had reached the tomb first also went in, and he saw and believed. (They did not yet understand the Scripture, that Jesus had to rise from the dead.) So the disciples returned to their homes, [wondering what had happened].

But Mary kept standing outside near the tomb, weeping. As she was weeping, she stooped down and looked into the tomb, where she saw two angels in white sitting where the body of Jesus had lain, one angel at the head and the other at the feet.

"Woman," they asked her, "why are you weeping?"

"Because they took away my Lord," she answered, "and I don't know where they laid him." After saying this, she turned and saw Jesus standing there. But she didn't know it was him.

"Woman," Jesus asked her, "why are you weeping? Who are you looking for?"

She thought he was the gardener. "Sir," she said, "if you carried him away, please tell me where you laid him, and I'll take him."

"Mary," Jesus said.

She turned toward him and said, "Rabboni!" (which means, "Dear teacher!").

The Resurrection

"Don't hold on to me," Jesus said to her, "for I haven't yet ascended to my Father. But go to my brothers and tell them, 'I am ascending to my Father and your Father, and to my God and your God.'"

Mary Magdalene went and told those who had been with him, as they mourned and wept, that she had seen the Lord and he had told her these things. But though they heard he was alive and that she had seen him, they did not believe it.

Joanna and Mary, the mother of James, and the other women with them came to the tomb when the sun had risen. They were discussing with each other, "Who will roll away the stone from the door of the tomb for us?" (It was very large.) But when they looked up, they saw that the stone was already rolled away.

When they entered the tomb, they did not find the body of the Lord Jesus. While they were wondering about this, they saw a young man sitting to the right, clothed in a long, white garment. They were startled. Then suddenly two men stood by them in dazzling clothes.

The women were terrified and bowed their faces to the ground. Then the angel said to them, "Don't be afraid; don't be overcome. I know you are looking for Jesus of Nazareth, who was crucified. Why do you look for the living among the dead? He isn't here because he has risen just as he said he would. Remember that he said to you while he was still in Galilee, 'The Son of Man must be handed over to sinful men, and be crucified, and on the third day rise again.'"

Then they remembered what Jesus had said. And the angel told them, "Come and see the place where the Lord was lying. But go quickly and tell his disciples—and Peter—that he has risen from the dead, and he is going ahead of you to Galilee. You will see him there just as he said you would. See, I have told you."

So they left quickly and fled from the tomb, trembling with astonishment. They said nothing to anyone because they were afraid. Then they ran to tell his disciples.

As they were on their way, Jesus met them and said, "Rejoice!" Then they came and grabbed his feet and worshiped him.

"Don't be afraid," Jesus said to them. "Go and tell my brothers to go to Galilee, and there they will see me."

They returned with utter joy and told all these things to the eleven apostles and to everyone else. But their words sounded like nonsense to them, and they didn't believe the women.

As the women were leaving, some of the soldiers entered the city and reported to the chief priests everything that had happened. After they had gathered with the elders and discussed the situation, they gave the soldiers a large sum of money and told them, "You are to say, 'His disciples came during the night and stole his body while we were asleep.' If the governor should hear about it, we will satisfy him and get you out of trouble."

So they took the money and did as they were told. To this day this story is widely spread among the Jews.

Jesus was later revealed in another way. That day two of them were walking into the country to a village named Emmaus, about seven miles from Jerusalem. They were discussing everything that had taken place. As they talked and reasoned, Jesus himself approached and walked with them. But they were kept from recognizing him.

He asked them, "What are you talking about with each other as you walk along with such sad faces?"

One, named Cleopas, answered, "Are you the only one staying in Jerusalem who doesn't know about the events that have happened there recently?"

"What things?" he answered.

"The things about Jesus of Nazareth, a prophet who was powerful in both deed and word before God and all the people. The chief priests and our rulers handed him over to be condemned to death by crucifixion. We were hoping it was he who would redeem Israel.

"What's more, this is the third day since these things happened, and today some women from our group astonished us. They were at the tomb early this morning and didn't find his body. They returned saying they had even seen a vision of angels who told them he was alive! Some of those who were with us went to the tomb and found it just as the women had said, but they didn't see him."

Then he said to them, "O foolish people who are slow of heart to believe everything the prophets spoke! Was it not necessary for the Messiah to suffer these things and then enter into his glory?" Beginning with Moses and all the prophets, he explained to them in all the Scriptures the passages about himself.

As they approached the village where they were going, he acted as if he would go farther. But they pleaded with him. "Stay with us," they said, "because evening is near and the day is almost gone." So he went in to stay with them.

As he reclined at the table with them, he took the bread and blessed and broke it and began giving it to them. Their eyes were opened, and they knew who he was. Then he vanished from their sight.

Jesus and the Disciples Going to Emmaus

They said to each other, "Didn't our hearts burn within us as he spoke with us on the road and kept explaining the Scriptures to us?"

That very hour they got up and returned to Jerusalem. There they found the eleven and those with them gathered together and saying to each other, "The Lord has really risen! He appeared to Simon!"

Then they told them what had happened to them on the road and how they had recognized Jesus when he broke the bread. But they didn't believe them.

It was evening on the first day of the week, and the disciples were assembled behind locked doors because they were afraid of the Jews. As they were talking, Jesus himself came and stood among them and said to them, "Peace to you!"

They were shocked and terrified and thought they were seeing a ghost. But he said to them, "Why are you alarmed? And why do doubts arise in your minds? Look at my hands and my feet—it is I myself. Touch me and see! A ghost doesn't have flesh and bones, as you see I have." When he had said this, he showed them his hands and feet and side.

Only then did the disciples become joyful at seeing the Lord. While they were still overwhelmed with wonder and disbelief because of their joy, he said to them, "Do you have anything here to eat?"

They gave him a piece of broiled fish [and a honey-comb,] and he ate in front of them.

Jesus then said to them, "Peace to you! As the Father has sent me, so I am sending you." Then he breathed on them and said, "Receive the Holy Spirit. If you forgive anyone's sins, they have been forgiven, and if you do not forgive anyone's sins, they have not been forgiven."

Now Thomas, also called Didymus, one of the twelve, was not with them when Jesus came. When the other disciples told him, "We have seen the Lord!" he replied, "Unless I see the imprint of the nails in his hands and press my finger into the mark of the nails and my hand into his side, I refuse to believe."

Eight days later the disciples were again indoors, and Thomas was with them. Although the doors had been locked, Jesus came and stood among them and said, "Peace to you!"

Then he said to Thomas, "Put your finger here and look at my hands, and take your hand and press it into my side, and stop doubting and believe."

Thomas answered, "My Lord and my God!"

"You have believed me," Jesus said to Thomas, "because you have seen me. Blessed are those who have not seen and yet have believed."

Afterward Jesus revealed himself to the disciples again, this time at the Sea of Tiberias. he did so in this way.

Simon Peter, Thomas (called Didymus), Nathanael of Cana in Galilee, the sons of Zebedee, and two other disciples were together when Simon Peter said, "I'm going fishing."

"We'll go with you," they replied. They left at once and climbed into the boat, but they caught nothing that whole night.

When morning had come, Jesus was standing on the shore, although the disciples didn't know it was Jesus. He said to them, "Children, do you have any fish?"

"No," they answered.

"Cast your net on the right side of the boat," he said, "and you'll find some."

After they cast the net, they couldn't pull it in because the catch was so large.

Then the disciple Jesus loved said to Peter, "It's the Lord!"

When Simon Peter heard it was the Lord, he put on his outer garment (which he had taken off) and threw himself into the sea. The other disciples came in the boat (they weren't far from shore, perhaps a hundred yards), dragging the net filled with fish.

When they reached the shore, they saw where a fire of coals had been built, with fish laid on top of it, and bread.

"Bring some of the fish you just caught," Jesus said.

Simon Peter went on board and pulled the net to shore, filled with 153 large fish. Even though there were so many, the net wasn't torn.

"Come and have breakfast," Jesus said to them.

Not one of the disciples dared ask him, "Who are you?" They knew it was the Lord. Jesus took the bread and gave it to them and did the same with the fish.

Now this was the third time Jesus was revealed to his disciples after rising from the dead.

When they had eaten breakfast, Jesus said to Simon Peter, "Simon, son of John, do you love me more than these?"

"Yes, Lord," Peter replied. "You know I love you."

"Feed my lambs," Jesus told him.

A second time Jesus said, "Simon, son of John, do you love me?"

Peter replied, "Yes, Lord! You know I love you."

"Shepherd my sheep," Jesus said.

For the third time Jesus said to him, "Simon, son of John, do you love me?"

Peter was grieved that Jesus asked the third time, "Do you love me?"

He answered, "Lord, you know all things. You know I love you."

"Feed my sheep!" Jesus answered. "I'm telling you the truth, when you were younger, you dressed yourself and walked wherever you wanted. But when you're old, you'll stretch out your hands and another will dress you and carry you where you don't want to go." He said this to indicate what kind of death Peter would suffer to glorify God. Then he told Peter, "Follow me."

Peter turned, and he saw coming after them the disciple Jesus loved (who at the supper had leaned toward Jesus and asked, "Lord, who is the one betraying you?"). When Peter saw him, he said to Jesus, "What about this man, Lord?"

Jesus answered, "If I want him to remain until I come, what does that matter to you? Follow Me!"

That is why the rumor spread among the believers that this disciple would not die. Yet Jesus didn't say he wouldn't die but only, "If I want him to remain until I come, what does that matter to you?" (This same disciple testifies to these things and wrote these things, and we know his testimony is true.)

Then the eleven disciples went to Galilee to the mountain specified by Jesus. When they saw him, they worshiped him, though some doubted.

Jesus approached them and said, "All authority has been given to me in heaven and on earth. Therefore go and disciple all nations, baptizing them in the name of the Father and of the Son and of the Holy Spirit and teaching them to obey everything I commanded you.

"And remember! I am with you at all times, until the very end of the age."

[Later he was revealed to the eleven as they met together for lunch. He then reproved them for their unbelief and stubborn hearts to believe the reports of his resurrection.

Then he said, "Go into all the world and preach the good news to the whole creation. Whoever believes and is baptized will be saved; those that refuse to believe will be condemned. Signs will accompany those who believe. In my name they will cast out demons, speak in new tongues, and even pick up snakes. If they drink any deadly thing, it will not hurt them. They will lay hands on the sick and they will recover.]

"The basic message I have given you," Jesus declared, "is this: everything written of me in the Law of Moses, the prophets, and the psalms must be fulfilled."

Then he opened their minds to understand the Scriptures. "Those writings," Jesus said, "have shown how necessary it was that the Messiah should suffer and on the third day arise from the dead. Repentance and forgiveness of sins must then be proclaimed in his name to all the nations, beginning at Jerusalem.

"You are witnesses of these things. But [you're not alone!] I am sending forth the promise of my Father upon you. Relax in the city of Jerusalem until you are clothed with power from on high."

After this final instruction, the Lord Jesus led them out to the vicinity of Bethany. There he lifted his hands and blessed them. As he was blessing them, he departed from them [and was received up into heaven. There he sat down at the right hand of God.]

In an attitude of worship, the disciples then returned to Jerusalem with great joy. There they continued in the temple, praising God. [As they later went out and preached everywhere, the Lord worked with them, confirming the message by miraculous signs that followed.]

Jesus also performed many other miracles in his disciples' presence that are not written down in this book. I suppose that even the world itself couldn't contain the books to be written if all these things were reported one by one. Amen.

But these have been written so you may believe that Jesus is the Messiah, the Son of God, and that by believing you may have life in his name.

᷍

MORE ABOUT
THE JESUS STORY

This Unique Translation

Since the second century AD, roughly 170 blended or harmonized versions of the Gospels have been published, a number of very good ones appearing in the twentieth century. But the blended version used in this book is unique for several reasons.

First, this version of the Gospels utilizes the "interweaving" method of harmonizing the four Gospels. Rather than laying out the four texts separately in parallel columns or horizontal lines, they are carefully interwoven to read as one complete story. Other versions of interwoven Gospels are often selective. When the Gospel writers report the same event, other versions may use the account with the most information while minimizing or omitting the contributions of the others. But wherever possible this version uses every word from every Gospel without adding a word in order to provide a complete and accurate story.

Second, this version has been thoroughly authenticated using English and Greek texts. Though they consulted more than twenty English translations, Johnston Cheney and Stanley Ellisen also checked the integrity of their work against the Greek text of the United Bible Society of 1966. The process of translating and authenticating was painstakingly and prayerfully completed over a period of twenty-three years. The fascinating story of Cheney and Ellisen's work is summarized below.

Third, the chronology of events in this narrative reflects Cheney and Ellisen's scholarly conviction that Jesus' earthly ministry covered a period of about four years instead of the traditionally accepted three years. The readings in this book are organized on this basis.

As you read through *The Jesus Story* you can be sure you are getting the whole story—every detail of Jesus' life and ministry as originally provided by the four Gospel writers, yet skillfully blended together into one narrative.

GOD'S INSTRUMENTS FOR
COMPLETING THIS TRANSLATION

Johnston M. Cheney was God's primary instrument for preparing this narrative. His story is an inspiring testimony of what can be accomplished through one person who is devoted to Christ and his word.

Growing up in the early twentieth century, Johnston Cheney planned to become a minister like his father. In college he specialized in English, the humanities, public speaking, and Greek, along with three years of Bible and theology. He showed exceptional talent in Greek. But one of Cheney's professors pointed out to him apparent contradictions in the Gospel accounts, contradictions that would undermine their historicity. Cheney was unable to refute the contradictions, and his once solid faith in the supernatural authority of the Scriptures crumbled. He abandoned preparation for the ministry and joined the army during World War I.

After the war, Cheney reestablished his faith in God and in the Bible through the ministry of a church in his hometown of Portland, Oregon. His devotion to God's Word was exemplary. He memorized about ninety of his favorite chapters in the Bible, taught adult Bible classes, and became president of the local chapter of the Gideons, an organization dedicated to Bible distribution. As the years went by, Cheney sensed that God was leading him to prepare a book that would help prove the true character of the Bible. But his business, family, and ministry left him little time to take on another project.

It took a bout with a deadly disease to launch Cheney into fulfilling the calling he had sensed. Shortly after World War II, he was diagnosed with a case of double tuberculosis. Confined to bed, he decided he would spend his last months of life studying the Scriptures in Greek. During this time he discovered that the three different accounts of Jesus' baptism in the Greek New Testament could be blended into a single narrative. Soon he began applying this process to other parts of the four Gospels.

Cheney's task of interweaving the Gospels remained little more than a sickbed hobby until he made significant discoveries. First, he became convinced from the Scriptures that Jesus' earthly ministry spanned four years instead of three. This discovery removed a number of difficulties in harmonizing the Gospels. Second, he found an excellent solution to the difficult task of blending the four accounts of Peter's denials. He determined that Peter actually denied the Lord at least six times—three denials before the morning rooster crowed once and three more times before it crowed a second time. These discoveries convinced Cheney that the Gospels were carefully designed by one Author.

Energized by these discoveries, Cheney experienced a measure of stability in his health. Growing in his devotion to the task of compiling Christ's life into a single narrative, he memorized nearly all of the four Gospels in the original Greek language from the *Textus Receptus*. After twenty years of work he showed his blended translation to Dr. Earl Radmacher, then president of Western Theological Seminary in Portland, Oregon. Deeply impressed with Cheney's keen ability in the Greek of the Gospels, Radmacher connected him with seminary professor Stanley Ellisen, Th.D., a scholar in the life of Christ. Ellisen was similarly impressed with Cheney's unique translation. The two men labored side by side on the project for three more years. Ellisen's expertise as a scholar and editor proved to be invaluable to the book's first edition. At age seventy-six, Cheney learned how to operate a typesetting machine and set the type for the first edition himself.

Shortly after completing his work, Cheney suffered a stroke that left him unable to speak. Assured that his book would soon be published, he penned his final words to his family in his own hand: "I love you all." Then he passed into the presence of the Lord whose story he had labored so long to tell in a simple and seamless way.

The first edition of Cheney and Ellisen's blended Gospels was published by Western Seminary in 1969 under the title *The Life of Christ in Stereo*. A subsequent edition, entitled *The Greatest Story*, was published by Multnomah Books in 1994. Dr. Ellisen skillfully shepherded the book through revisions over the years. And Dr. Earl Radmacher remained a staunch advocate for the work through its various stages. These first two editions of the book are now out of print.

But one man was not content to allow Cheney and Ellisen's excellent translation to disappear. Robert A. Meltebeke, Dr. of Ministry, an acquaintance of Ellisen and Radmacher, acquired the rights to the blended translation. Enlisting Ellisen's help, Meltebeke published another edition of the work entitled *Jesus Christ, The Greatest Life* (Paradise Publishing, 1999), including a leader's guide and study guide. Shortly after completing his work on this edition, Dr. Ellisen passed away.

In early 2015 Bill Perkins approached Dr. Bob and Sara Meltebeke about creating a unique version of the blended Gospels in which the four Gospels could be read like a novel, without chapter and verse references, footnotes, endnotes or commentary. Bill's desire to publish such a book flowed from his reading of the blended Gospels for over 30 consecutive months. Dr. Melbebeke and Sara agreed that such a version would be unprecedented and would provide readers with a unique way to experience the story of Jesus. And so the version of the blended Gospels you're holding came to life.

Cover and Interior Design by
Faceout Studio, Emily Weigel

Interior Illustrations by
Gustave Doré

Title and headers set in Neutraface 2 Text
Body copy set in Garamond MT

Cloth wrap: Arrestox B French Roast
Paper stock: Sebago IV Antique CW